The Day of War

Practical applications for spiritual warfare

Allen Porter

WestBow
PRESS
A DIVISION OF THOMAS NELSON

Unless otherwise noted Scripture quotations taken from the Holy Bible, New Living Translation, copyright 1996, 2004. Used by permission of Tyndale House Publishers, Inc., Wheaton, Illinois 60189. All rights reserved.

WestBow Press books may be ordered through booksellers or by contacting:

WestBow Press
A Division of Thomas Nelson
1663 Liberty Drive
Bloomington, IN 47403
www.westbowpress.com
1-(866) 928-1240

ISBN: 978-1-4497-1820-6 (sc)

Library of Congress Control Number: 2011930147

Printed in the United States of America

WestBow Press rev. date: 6/2/2011

CONTENTS

Introduction   vii
Chapter 1   The unseen world   1
Chapter 2   The Strategy of "Do"   9
Chapter 3   Taking Your Stand   15
Chapter 4   Rules of Engagement   25
Chapter 5   The Belt of Truth   39
Chapter 6   The Breastplate of Righteousness   48
Chapter 7   The shoes of peace   52
Chapter 8   The Shield of Faith   57
Chapter 9   The Helmet of Salvation   63
Chapter 10 The Sword of the Spirit   72
Chapter 11 Prayer   80
Conclusion   105

INTRODUCTION

We live in a day of war. Throughout history, the word "day" has been used to refer to a measure of time. An example would be the day of the horse and buggy. Of course, this is not to imply that we only used horse and buggy for one day. It is a term we use when referring to the days of the horse and buggy era. The term "Day of War" is more than just a book title. It illicits a significant question. How long does this war last? The short answer to this question is; until we see Jesus; either returning to the earth as King or until we see Him face to face which will occur immediately after we draw our last breath. The term "Day of War" is telling us to prepare for a long campaign. Too often people have experienced victory and thought the war was finally over. They had not in fact won the war, but a significant battle in the war. When you win a battle celebrate it, but keep your armor on and stay alert, because we live in a "Day of War".

You are in this war whether you like it or not. There is no avoiding it. You may object to it. You may say it is not fair. You may choose not to fight, but your enemy's intent is to kill, steal and destroy everything you hold dear. 1 Peter 5:8 says, "Be self-controlled and alert. Your enemy the devil prowls around like a roaring lion looking for someone to devour." John 10:10 also says: "The thief cometh not, but for to steal, and to kill, and to destroy. " This war started long before you got here and, unless Jesus returns before hand, will continue long after you leave. Our enemy in this war is Satan. Ignoring him only empowers and encourages him. You cannot make a treaty with him. Many people have believed the lie, that if you simply leave him alone he will not hurt you. The exact opposite is true. Your passive life will attract your enemy as he searches for an easy score. Your best choice is to learn about your enemy. Understand his power and resources. Then look at your own ability. When you do this, you are going to recognize that you need help. That is where Jesus is waiting to equip you with the armor and the battle plan that has already sealed the doom of your enemy.

This book is based on Ephesians chapter six. We will rely heavily on this passage to gain understanding about this war and how to win day by day. In order to thoroughly understand Ephesians chapter six it would be helpful to read the entire book of Ephesians. Ephesians six is one of the best-known passages of scripture in the Bible. Those of you who grew up in church can remember lessons and sermons about the armor of God. However, the book of Ephesians is not about armor or our enemy or even about spiritual warfare. It is a book about Jesus. The key phrase in the book is, "in Christ". Our focus will be chapter six. This chapter talks about the armor. You will learn that the armor belongs to God and it will only fit Christlike warriors. As you read this book, you will discover that we do not begin talking about the armor until much later in this book. This is not unlike any type of combat training. Whether you are training to be a police officer or a combat soldier the training begins with learning who you are, how much authority you have, where it comes from, who you are fighting for, what your mission is, who your enemy is and how he fights. When you have a complete and thorough understanding of the elements then the weapons are introduced. Far too often in spiritual warfare, we look at things that seem small as unimportant and focus on the sensational things. Going on an overseas mission trip, for many is a once in a life time experience. It is sensational and worthwhile. However it is not more important than being a good witness at work or school on a daily basis. Many small things are significant. In battle there are sensational things that happen. In most cases these sensational things occur because of attention, or lack there of, to the significant things. Daily prayer and time in the Bible are significant. When we focus on the sensational at the cost of paying attention to the significant Satan will put on quite a show for us and use the very things we intended to defeat him to mislead us and destroy our faith.

So break out your Bible and read Ephesians. Consider it chapter one of this book.

Chapter One

The unseen world

Ephesians 6:12 "For we are not fighting against people
made of flesh and blood, but against the evil rulers and
authorities of the unseen world, against those mighty powers
of darkness who rule this world, and against wicked spirits
in the heavenly realms."

Imagine a battle scene. This scene is taking place deep in a jungle. There
are sounds of thunder as explosions occur all around. Bullets rip through
the palm branches as splinters from trees fly before your eyes. There are
cries of pain and agony, shouts of urgency and sometimes panic. Let your
mind go for a minute in all of this. Imagine the smell in the air. See if you
can feel the earth shake beneath your feet as a mortar shell explodes not
so far away. As the smoke clears from before your eyes, you see something
just ahead that looks strangely out of place. It is a small cradle. There is a
baby blanket carefully folded and draped over the edge. With curiosity,
you move stealthily up to the edge and peer into the bundle of blankets
and there to your surprise are . . . YOU!

With all the special effects, that Hollywood has to offer it is still
impossible to portray the violent spiritual warfare that has been going on
all around you since the moment of your conception. By the time you
reached your cradle, many who were conceived at the same time you were
had already been violently murdered in a process called abortion. Some
of you may have felt the tremors of shock as your mother considered

whether she would carry you and give you life or end it. As you made your way through family issues, battles on the playground, struggles in the classrooms, conflicts in relationships and all the other noises of life, you learned how to react and respond mostly by what you could see and feel with you five senses. Yet many of the things you can see and feel are driven by spiritual conflicts in the unseen world. Ephesians 6:12 "For we are not fighting against people made of flesh and blood, but against the evil rulers and authorities of the unseen world." (NLT)

I once rented a home that had a plum tree planted close to the drive where we parked our car. This home was in California where the climate was ideal for the tree to produce fruit nearly year around. These plums were not good to eat. The tree was a beautiful purple color and had been planted for its aesthetic value. We hated this tree. The plums would fall off by the dozen. It was impossible to get to the front door without stepping on them. They would stain the carpets in our cars. They would track up the tile in our entryway and, if you were not careful at times, stain our clothing. We were tenants and not homeowners at the time. It was not our choice to cut down the tree, so we were left to deal with the fruit. My son and I would shake the tree and sweep up all the plums, but no matter how hard we worked, the tree could outproduce our efforts. Our struggle with the plum tree provides a perfect picture of trying to fight spiritual battles in the natural. It is like pulling the fruit of a tree instead of taking an axe to its root. You have heard of, "getting to the root of the problem." The root is unseen. When fighting the battles of life always remember. "The things I can see with my physical eyes are often a distraction. The things that I cannot see are most significant in this war."

Imagine a co-worker. She dislikes you and is always looking for ways to disrupt your day. Several times, she has made you look bad in front of management and other co-workers. She has lied about you and done things that you simply could not understand. Can you imagine this scenario? This person has targeted you. You did not ask for this. Non-the–less, you cannot simply ignore it and responding to her directly only makes you look petty as the two of you lock up in a power struggle. In most cases like this, both of you are destined to lose. How can you bypass the things you can see and get to the root of this problem? How do you seize the truth and power of Ephesians 6:12 and get to the real, unseen issues in this conflict? There are spiritual repercussions from this conflict that could last a lifetime. This is no time to be pulling fruit of the tree. It is time to be strong, suit up with you armor and win the fight!

2 Corinthians 10:3 "We are human, but we don't wage war with human plans and methods. 4 We use God's mighty weapons, not mere worldly weapons, to knock down the Devil's strongholds. 5 With these weapons we break down every proud argument that keeps people from knowing God. With these weapons we conquer their rebellious ideas." (NLT)

Always remember, God weapons are not designed to be used against people. You cannot strike a human being with the Sword of the Spirit any more than you can shoot the devil with a gun. You may not think of a conflict with a co-worker as war, but consider the potential impact of this conflict. It will affect the quality of your work. This can bring consequences ranging from how much you are paid to whether you keep your job. It will affect your family in many ways. How you interact with your family after a long day of conflict will have a long-term impact on them. It will affect your health. Stress and frustration are proven to have a serious impact on our physical and mental health. One definition of war is, "active hostility or contention; conflict; contest." When you carefully consider the potential damage that this circumstance can produce, how can you consider it anything less than war?

The most powerful factor in any war is the cause. What are you fighting for? Do you believe in what you are fighting for, or is it just an impulse? Impulses and emotions fade. However, a person who fights for a cause they believe in with all their heart will fight to their death. An example of people fighting with a cause can be seen in the Soviet-Afghanistan War. In 1978, the Soviet Union invaded Afghanistan with the intention of making Afghanistan part of the Soviet Union. The Mujahideen resistance fought this Communist super power in a way that the Soviets could not understand. The Mujahideen were outnumbered. Their weapons were inferior. They did not have adequate funding, but their cause was more powerful than all of the military might of Soviet Union. In February of 1988 after 10 years of war, the Soviet Union withdrew its forces from Afghanistan. This tiny, poverty-stricken country had defeated a giant. When it was all over, the tanks, plans, guns, bombs and numbers of warriors were no match for the strength of the Mujahideen. Their strength was not visible! If the soviets could have seen this invisible asset, they could have predicted their own defeat. This is a clear, modern day example of the invisible prevailing over the visible.

Now let us return to that conflict with a co-worker. What is the cause? What are you fighting for? If you are not careful, you will enter a world of revenge and selfishness as you fight for superiority. You will be tempted to manipulate and scheme in order to establish a carnal dominance. If you succeed, pride will surely enter in. If you fail, there will be humiliation and despair. If you focus on selfish things and ignore spiritual things your motives will be wrong and you will fight with human plans and not with God's mighty weapons. Both you and the co-worker will be puppets in a spiritual battle that cannot be seen with human eyes. Both of you will suffer loss.

So what is your cause? Jesus can help you with this answer. He has encountered problems exactly like this. His cause was single. His motive was always pure. 1 John 3:8 tell us, that the reason Jesus came was to destroy the works of the devil. Pay careful attention to the topic in this verse. Jesus did not come to destroy the devil. He came to destroy the works of the devil. Jesus knew something that so many would-be spiritual warriors never discover. Satan is a defeated foe! Satan was utterly defeated before Jesus ever came to planet earth. He was a defeated foe in the garden as he deceived Adam and Eve. He did not change his destiny by tricking Adam and stealing his birthright. Satan is an eternal being. God created him that way. God defeated Satan before mankind was created.

Saddam Hussein was soundly defeated in Dessert Storm. When he could see that his defeat was imminent, he set fire to the oil fields in his country. He did not change his destiny. He did not, in any way help his chance of prevailing in the war. His were the vengeful actions of a conquered leader. We still had to deal with his works, but his ability to win had been completely annihilated. Often, in a sporting event the outcome is sealed long before the game is over. Be careful! A defeated opponent is often more dangerous, once he can forecast his own defeat. Personally, I don't believe Satan is capable of knowing he is defeated because the Bible says there is no truth in him. This does not change the fact that Satan has lost, being thoroughly and eternally beaten! His doom is inevitable. Nothing he can do will change that. So we must do as Jesus did as He walked on the earth. We must focus on destroying the works of the devil.

What are these works? In the scenario of the conflict with the co-worker, we see some of his handywork. Jealousy, strife, bitterness, selfish ambitions, just to name a few. If you are going to be Christlike in this conflict, your goal will be to destroy the works of the devil and not those of the co-worker. Remember, Jesus wants to save you and the co-worker. He gave His life for both of you. If you take up His motive and His cause, you will win this conflict.

John chapter eight gives us one of the most beautiful stories in the Bible. In this story, we see Jesus dealing with a conflict that has some resemblances to the conflict with the co-worker. The big difference is that the intent of those opposing Jesus was to bring about His death. Much attention is given to Jesus' love and compassion toward the adulterous woman, but I want to look at Jesus' love and compassion for the Pharisees.

Jesus had gone through two significant encounters with this group of men over the past few weeks. The first is recorded in Matthew 9:9-13 9 As Jesus went on from there, He saw a man named Matthew sitting at the tax collector's booth. "Follow Me," He told him, and Matthew got up and followed Him. 10 While Jesus was having dinner at Matthew's house, many tax collectors and sinners came and ate with Him and His disciples. 11 When the Pharisees saw this, they asked His disciples, "Why does your teacher eat with tax collectors and sinners?" 12 On hearing this, Jesus said, "It is not the healthy who need a doctor, but the sick. 13 But go and learn what this means: I desire mercy, not sacrifice. For I have not come to call the righteous, but sinners." (NLT)

Only a few days later the Pharisees attempted to find fault with Jesus and His disciples again in Matthew 12: 1 At that time Jesus went through the grain fields on the Sabbath. His disciples were hungry and began to pick some heads of grain and eat them. 2 When the Pharisees saw this, they said to Him, "Look! Your disciples are doing what is unlawful on the Sabbath," 3 He answered, "Haven't you read what David did when he and his companions were hungry? 4 He entered the house of God, and he and his companions ate the consecrated bread--which was not lawful for them to do, but only for the priests. 5 Or haven't you read in the Law that on the

Sabbath the priests in the temple desecrate the day and yet are innocent? 6 I tell you that one greater than the temple is here. 7 If you had known what these words mean, 'I desire mercy, not sacrifice,' you would not have condemned the innocent." (NIV)

In the second encounter, Jesus reminded the Pharisees of the assignment He had given them only few days earlier. He was directing them to Micah 6:8. Now, in John chapter eight these same men have set themselves against Jesus again. This time, they intend far more than a simple confrontation. Their goal was to trap Jesus in a contradiction, accuse Him of blaspheme and incite the crowd to stone him. They rudely interrupt Jesus as He is teaching. They throw this woman at His feet, laid out their trap and waited for His response. Jesus had all the power of heaven at His disposal. He could have dealt with these men any way He wanted to. How would you have handled this conflict? Jesus' response was quiet and humble. He stooped and wrote in the sand. Over the years, there have been many guesses as to what Jesus wrote. What He wrote was not nearly as telling as why He did it. I believe He wrote something about mercy. He had been trying to teach them about mercy for weeks. I believe He wrote in the sand in an attempt communicate with these men without embarrassing them. I believe He knew how this chess match was going to end and was attempting to save these men from being humiliated. You and I might have enjoyed the fate of these men on this day, but Jesus loved them. He was trying to save them too! He wanted to set them free, just as He set that woman free that day. Jesus knew His cause! He knew these men were not His enemy. His cause was to set the captive free. His single motive in this conflict was to save as many as He could. When the Pharisees approached that day, Jesus was advancing His kingdom. As they attacked Him, He never faltered. He continued His work.

Your actions may not save the co-worker, but if they are Christlike, they will advance His kingdom. Advancing the Kingdom of God must always be your cause, if you are to wear His armor.

A few years ago as I was making final preparations to preach on Ephesians six, the Holy Spirit posed this question to me. "Why does God require His children to be strong?" At first, I dismissed this question, but the Holy Spirit repeated it and then gave me this revelation. The "why," will determine what kind of strength we develop. Track and field has many events. Each athlete will train and develop strength for his or her particular event. It is vital that he or she know why he or she is in the weight room. The "why," will dictate what kind of strength he or she develops. God's armor will not fit you if you develop the wrong kind of strength. Saul's armor would not fit David. It would not fit because David had not developed physical strength. His strength was spiritual. It could not be seen in the natural. It was demonstrated by what he shouted out to Goliath as they approached each other for this epic battle.

1 Samuel 17: 45 David shouted in reply, "You come to me with sword, spear, and javelin, but I come to you in the name of the LORD Almighty – the God of the armies of Israel, whom you have defied. 46 Today the LORD will conquer you, and I will kill you and cut off your head. And then I will give the dead bodies of your men to the birds and wild animals, and the whole world will know that there is a God in Israel! 47 And everyone will know that the LORD does not need weapons to rescue His people. It is His battle, not ours. The LORD will give you to us!"

Look at verse 46. God conquered and David demonstrated it by cutting of Goliath's head. This reinforces the lesson that Satan is already defeated. Cutting off the head demonstrates the loss of authority.

When we realize the truth, that Satan is already defeated, it helps us to keep everything in perspective. When we experience victory we always know why. We always stay humble and we always remember that the cause is setting free those who are captive. Over the years many foolish things have been said and done in the name of spiritual warfare. With human eyes and instincts it is impossible to determine what is foolish and what is serious. During my years in ministry I have witnessed demonic manifestations. For some people this is fascinating. It is like a real life scary movie. For others, who do not believe demons are real, it is all non-since. For a humble, spirit-lead warrior a demonic manifestation is a last desperate attempt of a demon who is resisting the will of God. The demon wants to be the main attraction. The Spirit lead warrior knows the main attraction is Jesus and the main goal is advancing the Kingdom of God.

In Luke chapter 10, as the 70 returned, they reported all the great works they were able to do in Jesus' name. As they gave this report they said, "even the demons were subject to us in Your name." The way they reported this experience indicates that, for these people, the highlight of the event was that demons were subject to them. Jesus warned them not to rejoice about the demons, but rather that their names were written in the Lamb's Book of life. Once again look at what Jesus was focused on and make that your focus. One hundred years from now, we will not be celebrating Satan's defeat. We will be celebrating Jesus' victory. We will celebrate the lives and the salvations of our fellow saints. We live in a day of war. The outcome is certain. Our mission is to destroy the works of the devil. His works are devices that hold men and women in captivity. The fight is not to defeat Satan or inflict some type of punishment on him. He is an obstacle in the way of the prize. Our focus must always be on the prize.

When, the book of Ephesians tells us to be strong in the Lord's mighty power, we must remember why He instructs us to be strong. We are to be strong so we can take souls away from the devil. Our strength is not one of defense. The armor is not to protect my health, my wealth or my family. God does that! The armor is designed for offence, not defense. Jesus said that the gates of hell would not prevail against His Church. Gates are not a portable weapon. Jesus was foretelling the location of our battle. We are to be at the gates of the enemy, not at home defending our stuff, but on Satan's turf, destroying his works and setting free those he has taken captive. We are not looking for demons. We are looking for captives in need of the good news! We are not focusing on defeating the devil. We are focusing on setting free those whom Jesus died to save! When the desire to see the Kingdom of God established governs our motives, we will prevail in every conflict. When we look at that co-worker the way Jesus looked at the Pharisees, we are able to put on His full armor. When we are suited up in this armor WE ARE UNBEATABLE!

CHAPTER TWO

THE STRATEGY OF "DO"

1 Chronicles 28:10 "So take this seriously. The LORD has chosen you to build a Temple as his sanctuary. Be strong, and do the work."

Love and hate are two forces in the human experience that are strong enough to compel people to lay down their lives. The suicide bombers on 9/11 were driven by hatred. Multitudes of missionaries have given their lives for the kingdom of God. These missionaries were driven by love. In both cases, these people were engaged in the action of doing something. They were both fighting a war. One fought for their god with hatred and anger. The other fought for Jesus with love and joy. Their lives were not defined by their abstinence. They are remembered for what they did. Far too often religion defines success by abstinence. When our focus is based on abstinence we judge our life based on what we don't do. "Thou shalt not" is far too often the trademark of Christianity. Abstinence is a defensive stance and will eventually fail if not reinforced with the affirmative action of doing.

Imagine standing before God and giving an account of your life. A person might say, "I did not steal. I did not covet my neighbor's wife, not one time ever! I did not bare false witness against any one." That person might go on at length along this line. When this person finishes listing all the things he did not do, I imagine what God would say is, "That is all fine and good, but what did you do?" In the end it will not be about the "don'ts" it will be about the "do's." In fact, most often doing the "do's" will be the key to abstaining from the "don'ts." Most of the time the sin of omission is the root cause of the sin of commission.

Matthew 25:31-46 records the parable of the sheep and the goats. This parable reinforces the importance of "doing." The parable tells how the Judge pronounced sentence on the goats because they failed to help various people in need. He then praises the sheep for their actions. The sheep had, no doubt made some mistakes along the way, but the mistakes were not mentioned. The mistakes had already been judged at Calvary! The single focus was their affirmative actions.

Simply stated, focus on doing what is right instead of abstaining from what is wrong. Abstinence is defense. Doing, is offence. In a game, it might be true that the best offence is a good defense, but in war, if you are playing defense you are losing! For a clear picture of this, let us go back to the Garden of Eden.

Eden was a beautiful garden prepared by God for His man. This garden is symbolic of our relationship with God. At the heart of this garden are two trees, the tree of life and the tree of knowledge of good and evil. Stop and think about this for a moment. What did God tell Adam concerning the tree of knowledge of good and evil? If your answer is, don't eat from this tree, you are set to make the same mistake that Adam made. You are destined to live in a legalistic world that will bring bondage. Your will live in a constant contradiction with the very first command that God gave to the human race. When God instructed Adam concerning this tree, His focus was not "don't", but "do!" Let's look at this scripture. Genesis 2:16 "And the Lord God commanded the man, 'You are free to eat from any tree in the garden; 17 but you must not eat from the tree of the knowledge of good and evil, for when you eat of it you will surely die.'" (NIV)

The command was, be free! Eat the good stuff! If Adam had done the "do," then, when he stood at the tree of knowledge of good and evil, he would have had a full stomach. Filled to the point of satisfaction, the tree would have had little attraction to him. It is also helpful to understand that without this tree, he would have had no choice. Without choice, his will could not have been activated. He would not have been able to obey the command to be free. Adam saw this tree as a tree of constraint, which contradicted his God given desire to be free. In truth, the tree of knowledge of good and evil was a tree of freedom, because it gave him a choice to serve God or rebel. Without this single and simple choice, Adam would not have been free. His freedom then and our freedom now are based on the action of "do." There is a time and place to practice abstinence, but our overall view of life should be about the "do's" and not the "don'ts." Our strength to abstain will come from our engagement of "doing."

1st Chronicles 28 records the powerful conclusion of King David's life and ministry. God has chosen Solomon to replace David as King. David is in the final hours of his life. His body temperature is falling. His vitals are dropping and all the other signs are indicating that his death is imminent. Like the great warrior he had always been, he continued moving forward with plans and strategies. David's last instruction to his son is recorded in 1st Chronicles 28:10.

So take this seriously. "The LORD has chosen you to build a Temple as his sanctuary. Be strong, and do the work."

The Hebrew word for "do" is "asah." It is a power-packed little word. The definition for this word is lengthy. Some of the definitions of this word include the following: to appoint, ordain, institute and to acquire (property). Solomon's instruction was to build God's Temple. Our instruction is the same. Solomon's temple was built with stone and furnished with treasure. Much of the material needed to build this temple had been taken by his father David in battle. Temple building today is done the same way. The kingdom of God is made up off lost souls that have been recovered in battle. These lost souls, once recovered become living temples for God.

2nd Corinthians 6:16 "For we are the temple of the living God." As God said: "I will live in them and walk among them. I will be their God, and they will be My people. (NIV)

We are fighting for souls. As we take them away from the kingdom of darkness and bring them into the kingdom of light, we are building God's temple. Temple building is our affirmative action. It is what we DO!

Look at David's final instruction to Solomon. Be strong, and do the work. Spiritual warfare is hard work. Much of what we have called spiritual warfare is nothing more than temporary emotion, produced by motivational sermons. This is unproductive and dangerous. When you deliberately speak into the spiritual realm, you are going to get attention. Remember, this is war! I have witnessed first hand as people, under the influence of an emotional church service, call into the spiritual realm. They bind and they loose and they pull down strongholds. They speak loud and passionately and then they leave and go back to their daily routine. This is not spiritual warfare. It is foolishness. To be a true spiritual warrior you will need to develop strength. Ephesians 6:10 says, "Be strong with the Lord's mighty power." God's source of power in this world is His Word. By His Word, all that we know was created. John 17:17 says that his Word is truth. We are battling the father of lies. When Jesus was confronted by Satan in the wilderness, he defeated him with the Word of God.

When moved by a powerful sermon or some other experience, you may start a battle. You must understand that this battle will not be concluded in five or ten minutes at the altar. On Tuesday afternoon, long after the goose bumps have faded, the enemy that you engaged will still be occupied with his assignment. The same assignment you spoke against on Sunday. There is nothing casual about this battle to your enemy. He is passionate about this cause. The consequences for his failure are beyond anything you or I could possibly imagine. He will not accept defeat until he is broken beyond remedy. If you stand your ground, suited with God's armor, your victory is certain! But make no mistake. It will take hard work, God's strength, and a determination to see this battle through to the end.

Ephesians 6:11 tells us that our enemy has strategies and tricks. This is important information. Satan and his demons are not going about haphazardly in doing evil. They have strategies and tricks. Strategies are referred to as an art in many dictionaries. They are a result of study and discipline. An effective strategy has been refined by doing the same thing over and over while making adjustments to maximize its effectiveness. In most cases strategies are written out. The devil also has tricks. The basis of a trick is deceit. A trick is designed to manipulate by using deceit. The evil spirits we deal with in spiritual warfare are skilled in deceit. They have strategies to mislead us. Ephesians 6:11 tells us to put on the armor so we can stand against the strategies and tricks of Satan. There is one thing to know about this. The devil is a liar.

John 8:44 He (Satan) was a murderer from the beginning and has always hated the truth. There is no truth in him. When he lies, it is consistent with his character; for he is a liar and the father of lies.

The kingdom of darkness fights with one basic weapon. Lies! Satan has no time to waste, so these are not passive lies. Another way of saying it is these lies are not harmless. When he puts a thought in your mind, it will always be untrue. If you do not deal with it, it will take root, like a seed. It will grow and produce fruit.

2 Corinthians 10:4 states that the weapons we fight with are not the weapons of the world. On the contrary, they have divine power to demolish strongholds. In 10:5 we read that we demolish arguments and every pretension that sets itself up against the knowledge of God, and we take captive every thought to make it obedient to Christ.

To do this effectively will require a lifestyle. You cannot expect to be successful without being faithful in your walk. Your knowledge of the truth is your strength to overcome the lie. This truth begins with spending time in the Bible. A sermon on Sunday and a quick devotional two or three times a week does not constitute a spiritual warrior!

Doing will make you strong. Abstinence will burn you out. Doing is exciting. Abstinence is exhausting. Doing will give your life meaning, as you experience victory. Abstinence, by itself has no thrill of victory. In fact, often it will leave you feeling cheated as you watch others enjoy life. This feeling will lead to bitterness. It will make you judgmental of others. You will find yourself wanting to diminish others in order to validate your own efforts.

Cain gives us a clear picture of what this looks like. He was upset with the fact that God had accepted Abel's offering and rejected his. We read in Genesis 4:3 the following passage: "At harvest time Cain brought to the LORD a gift of his farm produce, 4 while Abel brought several choice lambs from the best of his flock. The LORD accepted Abel and his offering, 5 but he did not accept Cain and his offering. This made Cain very angry and dejected. 6 "Why are you so angry?" the LORD asked him. "Why do you look so dejected? 7 You will be accepted if you respond in the right way. But if you refuse to respond correctly, then watch out! Sin is waiting to attack and destroy you, and you must subdue it."

The King James version states that, "if you do well, you will be accepted." God goes on to tell Cain if you don't do what is right, then sin is waiting for you. This passage shows us that "doing" is the key! If you don't do, then sin is waiting to attack you. This is when we tend to practice abstinence. This is playing defense.

Earlier in this chapter I told you that effective spiritual warfare begins with spending time in the Word. This is step one. Spending time in God's Word will cause you to know Jesus better. As you get to know Him, instead of just knowing about Him, your love for Him will grow. You will spend more time with Him and you will begin to hear from Him. By the power of the Holy Spirit, you will hear clear instructions. He will instruct you by putting you in remembrance of the Word of God.

John 14: 26 "But when the Father sends the Counselor as my representative – (and by the Counselor I mean the Holy Spirit) – He will teach you everything and will remind you of everything I myself have told you."

Jesus said the Holy Spirit would remind you. The Holy Spirit cannot remind you of things of which you have no knowledge.

To conclude this chapter, let's consider what a person must do in order to put on God's armor. Remember, His armor will only fit Christlike warriors. The warrior who is ready to put on the whole armor is strong with God's mighty power. This person is well-versed in Scripture. Spending time with God is a daily priority. This leads to a deep understanding of the truth, which helps this person quickly identify any lie of the devil. This person is not fighting for his or her own selfish desire. He or she has made the Kingdom of God his or her primary concern. When he or she comes across a lie of the devil, he or she takes it captive and makes it submissive to God's will. He or she do this with his or her tongue! This topic will be talked about at length in the next chapters. The spoken word is your key to reaching the spiritual realm.

But before you reach for the sword of the Spirit, which is the Word of God, let us do just a little more preparation. Our preparation in God's word will make us champions in this day of war.

Chapter Three

Taking Your Stand

Ephesians 6:11 "Put on all of God's armor so that you will be able to stand firm against all strategies and tricks of the Devil. 12 For we are not fighting against people made of flesh and blood, but against the evil rulers and authorities of the unseen world, against those mighty powers of darkness who rule this world, and against wicked spirits in the heavenly realms. 13 Use every piece of God's armor to resist the enemy in the time of evil, so that after the battle you will still be standing firm. 14 Stand your ground,"

One of the most well known battles in American History is the Alamo. The men who fought in that battle give us a vibrant picture of what it means to take a stand.

On February 23, 1836, a Mexican troop of approximately 1,500 marched on this strategic military outpost, which was a small mission known as the Alamo. The Alamo had just over 100 men. Knowing their defeat was imminent, these men took their stand. Before the first shot was fired they had made a decision. They could have ran way. They could have attempted to negotiate. However, they decided to take their stand. All but two of the men who fought to defend the Alamo were killed, but their stand stirred the hearts of the Texan army and led to a lasting victory.

To take a stand is not a casual thing. It is an act of your will based on deep-seated beliefs. Only people of character are able to take a stand. These are people who will set aside personal comfort, selfish desire and in some cases even their lives for their beliefs and values.

Before you take a stand, be sure that the Holy Spirit motivates you rather than some emotion or noble cause. There are countless noble causes, but you cannot volunteer for a cause based on emotions and expect victory. If you are an emotionally driven person, the very thing that caused you to get into the battle in the first place, will be the reason for your surrender and defeat. Emotions are a part of the battle, but they can never be the driving force.

The next time you are inspired to volunteer for battle, think about the story of Jesus and the money changers in the temple. His calling and timing were two key factors in His decision to address this issue. For many years He endured the offense of the money changers in the temple. Jesus didn't just happen to notice this problem the day He cleansed the temple. This activity had roused His passion since He was a young boy, but His passion was subordinate to His call. When the time came, the call was given and Jesus' passion was unleashed! Notice that His passion was governed by His call. Jesus was clearly aware of the many serious issues of the day. There was major corruption in the Sanhedrin. The Roman government was evil. King Herod was a ruthless butcher. Poverty was everywhere, but Jesus carefully selected His battles, based on His calling. He did not try to solve all the problems of the day. What He did do was to listen carefully to what His Father told Him to do. Jesus knew true spiritual warriors are not volunteers. God chooses them, for a distinct purpose.

Revelation 17:14 "Together they will wage war against the Lamb, but the Lamb will defeat them because He is Lord over all lords and King over all kings, and His people are the called and chosen and faithful ones."

This scripture shows us that God's warriors were first called, and then chosen because of their faithfulness. When God has chosen you and assigned you to a battle, He will always provide you with the grace to win that battle. The victory is settled before the battle begins! To secure your place with the other victorious warriors, you must take your stand!

To better comprehend what it means to take your stand, let us take an in depth look at the Greek word the Apostle Paul used as he wrote Ephesians 6:13.

The word "stand" is translated from the Greek word, "histemia." Below is a comprehensive definition of this word.

Histemi (pronounced his'-tay-mee) a verb

Definition
to cause or make to stand, to place, put, set
to bid to stand by, [set up]
in the presence of others, in the midst, before judges,
to place, to make firm, fix establish
to cause a person or a thing to keep his or its place
to stand, be kept intact (of family, a kingdom), to escape in safety
to establish a thing, cause it to stand 1b
to uphold or sustain the authority or force of anything
to set or place in a balance
to weigh: money to one (because in very early times before the introduction of coinage, the metals used to be weighed)
to stand by or near
to stop, stand still, to stand immovable, stand firm 2a
of the foundation of a building
continue safe and sound, stand unharmed, to stand ready or prepared
to be of a steadfast mind
of quality, one who does not hesitate, does not waiver

Three things must happen for you to be successful in taking your stand. You must be called. You must be chosen and you must be faithful. Far too often, Christians, with the best of intentions, have embarked on battles without considering these three actions. The result of going to war without a call, without being chosen and without faithfulness will always be failure. We must approach the armor of God with a clear-headed understanding of the battle that lies ahead and set aside shallow "emotion-driven" ideals. As we are suiting up with God's armor, we are taking our stand. In our hearts, we know that we are called of God for this fight. We know that our all-knowing God, would never call us to a losing battle. Therefore, before we take up a single piece of the armor, we know the battle is ours!

The Call

Imagine a hostage situation at some busy office complex in a city. The police have arrived and the special units are setting up. Snipers are in place atop the surrounding buildings. The command post is operational. Reporters have taken their place and the scene is set for this stand off. Now imagine that right in the middle of this (this what? specify) a pickup truck pulls up. Three men get out with their hunting rifles and begin to make their way towards the office building where the hostages are. These men have not been called. Because they have not been called, they have no valid authority to be there. The misguided attempt of these men to save the day only increases the likelihood that someone is going to get hurt. These men have numerous deficiencies when it comes to dealing with this circumstance. First and foremost, they have not been called or chosen. Even as dozens of people have been called and deployed, there are many qualified personnel waiting for the call. It is easy to see that these three hunters are out of place. Even if one individual of the trained Special Forces shows up, that person will be out of place if he or she has not been called.

Now let's look at a biblical example:

Luke 22: 47 "But even as He (Jesus) said this, a mob approached, led by Judas, one of His twelve disciples. Judas walked over to Jesus and greeted Him with a kiss. 48 But Jesus said, 'Judas, how can you betray Me, the Son of Man, with a kiss?' 49 When the other disciples saw what was about to happen, they exclaimed, 'Lord, should we fight? We brought the swords!' 50 And one of them slashed at the high priest's servant and cut off his right ear. 51 But Jesus said, 'Don't resist anymore.' And He touched the place where the man's ear had been and healed him."

As we consider this passage, let's begin with the question, "Lord, should we fight?" With 2,000 years of history and a full understanding of what was going on, this question seems overly simple. If we were limited in our knowledge as the disciples were, this question would sound much different. Peter had no need for such a question. To him it seemed a foolish question. Based on what he could see and know, it was time to take action! Judas had also taken action. His intention was not the death of Jesus. His battle plan was to put Jesus on the spot and force Him to begin the revolution that would overthrow the Roman government. Judas and Peter took bold action that night. Much like the three men in the pickup, their actions were misguided. They had not been called or chosen. They were moving on their own, based on mere human knowledge. Without the correction that Jesus brought, by healing the person's ear, all the disciples might have been arrested and killed. The disciples were limited in their knowledge and their authority. Ten disciples were wise enough to ask, "Lord, should we fight?" They were waiting for the call. The two disciples who charged into the fight without the call suffered greatly.

When it comes to this day of war, each one of us have a call. God has not overlooked anyone. God has chosen to make you significant in this war. He has equipped you with unique talents that will be useful in advancing His kingdom. However, not everyone who answers the call will be chosen. The call goes out to many, bit only a few will be chosen. As God looks at the crowd of people who answer the call He is looking for a teachable heart. He is looking for humility. God will reject the *would be warrior* who shows up with his/her own ideas and plans. God is looking for a person with a heart like Moses or Gideon. These two men were not confident in their ability. This made them totally dependant on God. 2 Corinthians 12:9 tell us that it is in our weakness that God's power is perfected.

Matthew 22:9 "Now go out to the street corners and invite everyone you see. 10 So the servants brought in everyone they could find, good and bad alike, and the banquet hall was filled with guests. 11 But when the king came in to meet the guests, he noticed a man who wasn't wearing the proper clothes for a wedding. 12 'Friend,' he asked, 'how is it that you are here without wedding clothes?' And the man had no reply. 13 Then the king said to his aides, 'Bind him hand and foot and throw him out into the outer darkness, where there is weeping and gnashing of teeth.' 14 For many are called, but few are chosen."

The man in this story had rejected the king's garments and had decided that his were good enough. The king's servants would have advised him in this matter, but he rejected their advice and decided to do things his way. This kind of person is dangerous in battle. All of us are called, but only those who will listen and follow instructions will be chosen. Independent, know-it-all people, will be rejected. They may still choose to fight, but their action and the consequences will be like those of Peter and Judas, on the night of Jesus' betrayal.

When your heart is right, and your motives pure, God will make His call on your life clear. Sometimes the thing that keeps us from hearing the call is our own idea of what we want to do. Peter and Judas demonstrated what happens when we act on our own thoughts and plans with their actions on the night before Jesus' crucifixion. They would have done well to consider the words of the prophet Isaiah.

Isaiah 55: 8 " 'My thoughts are completely different from yours,' says the LORD. 'And My ways are far beyond anything you could imagine. 9 For just as the heavens are higher than the earth, so are My ways higher than your ways and My thoughts higher than your thoughts. 10 The rain and snow come down from the heavens and stay on the ground to water the earth. They cause the grain to grow, producing seed for the farmer and bread for the hungry. 11 It is the same with My word. I send it out, and it always produces fruit. It will accomplish all I want it to, and it will prosper everywhere I send it.' "

Often God's call will seem small. (Zechariah 4:10) When we answer the call, even though it seems small, we will then discover the truth of Luke 16:10. Unless you are faithful in small matters, you won't be faithful in large ones. If you cheat even a little, you won't be honest with greater responsibilities.

Before you finish this book, it is my prayer that you discover the call of God on your life. With this revelation you will be ready to take your stand in this day of war.

The Chosen and The Faithful

It is possible to be called, but not chosen. Consider the man who was invited to the wedding feast, but was later rejected for not changing into the wedding garments. Another real life example is recorded in Mark 10:17-21.

Mark10:17 "As he was starting out on a trip, a man came running up to Jesus, knelt down, and asked, 'Good Teacher, what should I do to get eternal life?' 18 'Why do you call Me good?' Jesus asked. 'Only God is truly good. 19 But as for your question, you know the commandments: Do not murder. Do not commit adultery. Do not steal. Do not testify falsely. Do not cheat. Honor your father and mother.' 20 'Teacher,' the man replied, 'I've obeyed all these commandments since I was a child.' 21 Jesus felt genuine love for this man as He looked at him. 'You lack only one thing,' He told him. 'Go and sell all you have and give the money to the poor, and you will have treasure in heaven. Then come, follow Me.' "

This man had a calling on his life. His calling brought him to Jesus. Jesus offered him a place in history, as well as answering his question about how to get to Heaven. The man lacked faith. He trusted in his wealth more than in Jesus. While it is possible for a person to be called , but not chosen, it is impossible for him or her to be chosen without being faithful.

There is no short cut to faithfulness. Romans 10:17 tells us that faith comes by hearing the word of God. The previous verse prior to that emphasizes obedience. James says it this way:

James 1: 22 "And remember, it is a message to obey, not just to listen to. If you don't obey, you are only fooling yourself. 23 For if you just listen and don't obey, it is like looking at your face in a mirror but doing nothing to improve your appearance. 24 You see yourself, walk away, and forget what you look like. 25 But if you keep looking steadily into God's perfect law – the law that sets you free – and if you do what it says and don't forget what you heard, then God will bless you for doing it. 26 If you claim to be religious but don't control your tongue, you are just fooling yourself, and your religion is worthless. 27 Pure and lasting religion in the sight of God our Father means that we must care for orphans and widows in their troubles, and refuse to let the world corrupt us."

As we move into the armor, you will discover that each piece of the armor is connected to the tongue. The things that dominate our thought life, becomes the things that we talk about. When you are faithful to spend time absorbing God's word, what you say will be impacted. When God's word dominates your thought, you will knock down strongholds as you go about your daily routine. You might not even be thinking about warfare, but your actions and your words will be destroying the works of the devil!

The Stand

As you search the scriptures, listen to sermons, read books and spend time in prayer, God's word will become part of who you are. Remember John 1:1. Jesus was called the Word! It is His will and plan to make us like Him. As we dedicate ourselves to His Word, we will find that the things we read are not just things we do, but it is who we are! It was not what Jesus did that changed the world. It was Who He was! When this is true of you then you will be ready to suite up with all the of God's armor!

When you are dressed for battle you appearance will give you confidence. As you take your stand, fully clothed in God's mighty armor your enemies will be in fear. Always remember, they are not afraid of you. They are afraid of your King and your Father! They know from ages past that they cannot prevail against a child of God fully clothed in the armor of God.

Take a moment and read Ephesians chapter six again. As you read it, let your imagination draw a detailed picture of what this warrior looks like. Look at their stance. Is it aggressive? Take a look in their face. What is their countenance like? Are they angry? Look this warrior in the eye. What do you see?

You might ask, why so much emphasis on this matter. The reason is that this entire passage of scripture is symbolic. When we are dealing with symbolic things in the Bible, it is very important that we are seeing the correct symbol. The picture on your left is a picture that many persons would accept as the armor the Apostle Paul was describing.

Medieval Knigh

There are many reasons why this picture cannot accurately relate what Paul was seeing as he described the armor of God. First, this type of armor and warrior did not exist. The previous picture is one of a medieval Knight. This type of armor and warrior would come centuries after Paul wrote Ephesians. The image Paul had is his mind as he wrote about the spiritual armor would have been shaped by what he had seen. Paul was under Roman guard at times. He had seen the occupying soldiers in Jerusalem. He had seen Hebrew soldiers as well. We will miss some of the meaning in this passage if we fail to see the image Paul was describing. Study the two pictures below and notice the differences.

Hebrew Warrior

Roman Warrior

The armor of the medieval Knight was cumbersome. It limited the warrior on where he could go and what he could do. The entire history the knight's armor was short-lived. The knight's armor could quickly become a liability. If the knight were knocked from his horse or if he fell in battle, the weight and bulk of his armor often made his recovery impossible. This armor was largely for defense. God's armor is designed for offense.

Remember the spiritual armor is not literal. It is symbolic. Paul is painting a detailed picture for us. If we envision a warrior that did not exist in his day, the picture we see is going to be different from the one he painted. This incorrect picture can be misleading and will certainly rob us of a full understanding of what the author was trying to convey.

The armor Paul described would have allowed the warrior "to be quick on his feet." He would have been able to recover quickly if he lost his footing. This armor was designed for offense.

Put on the full armor

What is the most important piece of armor? The answer is the one you are missing. Ephesians 6:13 tells us to use every piece of the armor. If you enter battle with only part of your armor, your enemy will be able to see clearly *(no comma here)* where you are vulnerable. Regardless of all the other armor, your weakness in battle is definite and obvious. Your enemy will quickly adjust his attack to exploit the area left unprotected. As you continue reading this book, pay close attention to every single piece of the armor. Only when you are suited with the full armor of God is your victory certain.

Chapter Four

Rules of Engagement

2 Corinthians 2:11 ...that Satan will not outsmart us. For
we are very familiar with his evil schemes.

In mid October 331 B.C., Alexander the Great captured Babylon. Just a
little over two months latter, he occupied Susa, unopposed. This marked
the fall of Persia to the Greeks. Alexander began the campaign that would
see the overthrow of the most powerful empire on earth with about 30,000
men. His success appeared unlikely to any reasonable person. The Greeks
had been fighting with the Persians for over 20 years. However, this
battle began in the spiritual realm 200 years prior to Alexander's military
campaign. In the physical realm, Philip II of Macedon started this war.
Phillip was the father of Alexander the Great. The apparent reason for
this conflict was manifold and complex. However, the true origin of this
conflict is documented in Daniel, Chapter 10. (It would be a good idea to
read this entire chapter before proceeding.)

Briefly stated, Persia fell because the demonic prince that ruled this
kingdom overstepped his authority and got between God and his man.
When the Prince of Persia refused to allow the angel to bring God's word
to Daniel, the conflict began that would bring about the end of this
empire.

This passage of scriptures gives you some incredible insight into the
invisible realm. Remember Ephesians 6:12 tells you that the fight is not
with flesh and blood, but against the evil rulers and authorities of the

unseen world, against those mighty powers of darkness who rule this world, and against wicked spirits in the heavenly realms. This story paints a vivid picture of what true spiritual warfare looks like. Daniel's quest for understanding provoked a conflict that would go on for over 200 years, resulting in the fall of one of the most powerful empires in history!

The Angel told Daniel in Chapter 10, Verse 12, "I have come because of thy words." (Young's Literal Translation) Consider this! The words of a Hebrew slave, had invoked a conflict that would wage in the spiritual world and spill over into the physical realm." This war would go on for over 200 years and would result in the overthrow of the most powerful kingdom on earth. All of this happened because a servant of God humbled himself and sought understanding concerning his people, Israel.

The role Daniel played in this incredible conflict is far different than that which most would-be spiritual warriors imagine today. Daniel did not stand and point to the heavens and cry out to the Prince of Persia, "I bind you." The fact is Daniel had very little idea what was going on. He was fasting and praying for understanding. After 21 days, Daniel received words from God that gave him the understanding for which he was searching. He then went on with his life.

Daniel never directly engaged the Prince of Persia. His lifestyle brought him into a place of conflict with this principality. He may have never had any direct knowledge of this prince, yet his words incited the battle that lead to the overthrow. This is one accept of spiritual warfare. There are times when we are going to have more understanding concerning the evil powers we are fighting. Even then, this story teaches us a lot about the rules of engagement.

In any military campaign, there are rules that govern how the soldiers fight. Each soldier has his role in the battle. If the soldier chooses a position or task that is not in his area of responsibility, he becomes a liability and will be removed from the battle.

Five simple rules of engagement.
1. The battle is the Lord's

Remember, in the beginning of this book you looked at the instruction to be strong in the Lord and His mighty power. Selfish ambition and desires often get in the way of this directive. When you began to fight for selfish reasons, you forfeit the armor. Often when this happens, you don't even realize it. You become like Sampson. (If you are not familiar with this story, it would be helpful to read Judges 16.) In Judges 16:20 Sampson had compromised his purpose and through a serious of mistakes he had lost God's power in his life. When the enemy came to take him away, he arose with confidence. In his mind he was ready for the fight. Based on past experience, he was certain he would prevail. The Bible relates that he did not know that the power of God had left him. As a result, this once mighty warrior, was defeated and taken captive. When he abandoned God's purpose for his life, he lost the power that came with it. That power did not return until the last moments of Sampson's life. At this point, he remembered what God had called him to do. He repented and stepped back into his appointed role. At that moment his power to fight was restored and he brought deliverance to God's people. This was his purposed assignment all along, but for many years Sampson had forsaken his assignment for selfish reasons. He had been fighting his battle and not the Lord's.

As you return once again to the example of the conflict with the co-worker from the first part of this book, you can see that the conflict with this person is physical. It is unavoidable. As this co-worker attacks you, you have no choice. You must respond. A passive response will have a negative impact on you. With this in mind you prepare to make your stand. Before you take any action, ask yourself this question, "What is the desired outcome?" Only one answer will make you suitable for battle. The purpose of every battle is to advance the Kingdom of God. If this purpose governs your actions in this conflict, you will always prevail. Staying on target is not easy. As personal attacks are made, it is easy to abandon your mission. Your emotions will tug and pull you to fight for your own selfish reasons. This puts you on a pathway of destruction. When you fight for any selfish reason, even when you win you loose.

Hezekiah demonstrates how you will be able to avoid the pitfall of fighting for selfish reasons.

The enemy does not fear you! He fears God's Word!

The reason Daniel's words were so powerful was that they lined up with God's will for his life. The Prince of Persia had no reason to fear

Daniel or anything that he might have to say, until Daniel's words aligned with God's will. If you have not prayed and spent time in the Bible, your words will have no power. A forty-five minute sermon does not equip you to take on a principality.

Take some time and study how Jesus engaged the demons. He didn't call them names. I do not believe He yelled and screamed at them. A demon is not moved by passion or presentation. He is moved by the Word of God. Jesus did not become distracted with anger for the demon, but remained focus on His love for the victim. This is not to say He was not angry, or that you should not be angry with the enemy, but anger has very little impact on the fight.

(Please don't misunderstand me. There are times when a fight gets emotional. I am not telling you not to raise your voice or show emotion. I am telling you that those actions will not be the decisive factor in winning the battle.)

The enemy will not obey you. He is only compelled by God's word. Often, in the heat of a spiritual battle things are said that demonstrate the warrior's lack of knowledge. Many times I have heard people command a demon to the pit of hell. While this often sounds majestic in the natural, it actually contradicts God's word. Not only do you not have the authority to make such a demand, the demon does not have the ability to comply. Satan and his angels will be cast into hell by the command of God at the end of this age. Having been expelled from heaven and exiled to earth by God, they have no choice in whether they stay or leave. You may compel them, by God's word, to leave this present location, but you have little say about where they go or what the final outcome will be.

When speaking into the spiritual realm, do not try to be elegant or witty. That is not the source of your strength. Instead, wait on the Lord. Ask the Holy Spirit for the right words. When you comply, your words will, most often be few and the power will be sufficient to win the battle. I often rely on the truth found in James 1:5. This verse tells you, if you lack wisdom, you need to ask God. It goes on to tell you that when you do He gives it to you abundantly. Even though I am writing a book on spiritual warfare, I am quick to admit my need for help when fighting in the unseen realm. My Father God knows every detail of every part of every fight! When I humble myself and wait for Him, He gives me insight and knowledge. By His Holy Spirit He helps me to say exactly the right thing. Many times in my life when the wisdom breaks through and I hear God's voice, it brings a quiet confidence and peace into my heart. In the midst of the battle, I have the confident assurance that the victory is already sealed! I have seen demons melt away with just a whisper at times. When I am under the control of the Holy Spirit, the softest whisper spoken from my home, here in Northern Iowa, can affect a battle in a Cambodian village, halfway around the world.

2. Remain humble at all times

Remaining humble is a constant vigil for any effective warrior. The qualities that make you willing to step on to the battlefield and fight also makes you susceptible to pride. Pride separates you from the truth that you can do nothing meaningful or worthwhile apart from God's power. It is His Truth, His Word, His Purpose. The battle belongs to the Lord! Apart from Him you will never win, but in Him you will never fail!

Pride often comes after a significant victory. Satan is right there to congratulate you and tell you what an awesome warrior you are. Sampson demonstrates this in Judges Chapter 14. In this chapter is the story of Sampson killing a lion, with his bare hands. Later Sampson returned to gaze upon the dead carcass. I believe pride drew Sampson back to the dead lion. This expedition, which was motivated by pride, turned a victory which had resulted from the power of God into a stumbling block for Sampson. His pride led him to commit two mistakes. First, Mosaic Law prohibited him from touching a dead corpse. When he saw the lion's corpse, he noticed that bees had built a hive in the lion's mouth. He took some of the honey and ate it, as well as giving some to his parents. The second mistake was made when he gave a riddle to his prospective in-laws. The riddle was based on his conquest of the lion. Sampson was completely self-absorbed in all of this activity. He stood to win goods from his wager. If no one could figure out his riddle, he would look wiser than his prospective in-laws and at some point he would be able to tell the story of how he had killed this lion with his own two hands. The Bible clearly says, the Power of the Lord came upon Sampson. This was no doubt a great victory. God's power saved Sampson's life. However, Sampson took credit for it and became proud. If you read this entire story, you will see that this event exploded into deadly consequences that would follow Sampson to his grave.

A wise warrior will pause at every victory and praise God. A wise warrior will be sure to give God all the glory for all his victories. Remember that James 4:6 tells you that God resists the proud, but gives grace to the humble. It is that grace that makes you able to win great battles.

When thoughts of greatness come into you in mind, begin to worship God for all greatness. Read Psalms aloud and you will defeat pride before it comes and steals the victory away from you.

The drama you see in the movies and TV shows may give you some idea of what war is like in the physical realm. The battles are epic and the warriors bigger than life. The music is played and people stand in awe, as the warrior draws upon his skill to overcome unbelievable odds. These make-believe characters are nothing like the spiritual warriors in the Bible. Men like Moses and Daniel or women like Ruth or Esther were often quiet and reserved. They knew their short-comings and relied wholly on the power of God for their success. There were those like David and Sampson. There was nothing quiet or reserved about these men, but their strength often became their weakness, as they relied on their own power. On the day that David fought Goliath, he boldly proclaimed, "The Lord will give you into my hand." This same man took a census of his army, against the instruction of God. It was a humble boy with a sling and the word of God that killed the giant. (1 Samuel 17) It was a King looking at the size and strength of his own army that brought about one of the most significant losses of his life. (2 Samuel 24) In this contrast, we see one man move with humility to defeat a giant. We later see this same man, moved by pride to take matters into his own hands with deadly results.

3. Know whom you are fighting.

Ephesians 6:12 identifies different entities that you and I war against. People often identify Satan as the entity they are fighting. You might hear some one say, "Satan, in the name of Jesus I command you …" What we must understand is that Satan is a fallen angel. While he wants very much to be like God, the fact is he is not like God in any way. He is not omnipresent. This is to say that he can only be in one place at a time. He is the commander of all the fallen angels and our fight is indeed with him.

However, most of us will never deal directly with Satan. Every soldier, who fought against the Nazis, fought against Hitler. Very few of those involved in the war against Hitler ever had a direct encounter with him. They encountered his soldiers but with every battle they were fighting against Hitler. We are fighting Satan. Most of us will never have a direct encounter with him. We are fighting his demons. As we encounter these spiritual enemies, we will find some weak and easy to defeat and some fierce and persistent. In most cases where Jesus dealt with demons openly, they melted away. There were occasions where the battle required more. Mark Chapter five, shows us an instance where demons actually argued with Jesus. He still prevailed. The demons in this man were so powerful that upon leaving the man, they entered a herd of 2,000 pigs and drove all of them over a cliff. A little wisdom will lead one to conclude that only someone truly serious about his or her faith should mess with a force like this. It is not my goal to scare any one away from the fight. I want to encourage you to fight. I want you to know that you can win every time, but I want you to take it seriously. This is not some sensational game to play for goose bumps and thrills. It is a war to fight for the lives of souls!

4. It's a war of words.

The most powerful force on this planet is the word. Words are how you form your thoughts. Words are how you convey thoughts to others. Nothing happens on this earth that is not driven by words. In Genesis 11 you can read about the Tower of Babel. This event helps to paint a picture of the power of words. As God looked down on this great structure He made a comment.

Genesis 11:6 "And the LORD said , 'Behold, the people is one, and they have all one language; and this they begin to do : and now nothing will be restrained from them, which they have imagined to do . 7 Go to, let us go down, and there confound their language, that they may not understand one another's speech.'" (KJV)

It was the spoken word that allowed them to begin this great task. As God observed this activity He made an amazing statement. "Nothing will be restrained from them, which they can imagine to do." He then reduced their capacity to imagine by confusing their language.

Take some time to think this over. Consider the power of words. I can affect a persons body chemistry, simply by saying certain words. Describe a slice of hot juicy pizza and you can make other people's mouth water. Describe the smell and taste of rancid milk and some people will become ill. Words can stir fear, hate or love. Wars begin and end with words.

This truth has been twisted by many hyper-faith movements over the years. Many have taken this truth to extremes. Always remember God remains sovereign in all of this. He is in charge. He sees all, know all and our own understanding is very limited. Our words, while they are powerful, have limits. However, when we search the heart of God on a matter and say what He wants us to say, we can in fact move mountains!

Matthew 17:20 "for verily I say unto you, If ye have faith as a grain of mustard seed, ye shall say unto this mountain, Remove hence to yonder place; and it shall remove; and nothing shall be impossible unto you." (KJV)

Words come in three forms. There is the written word. Our thoughts are made up of silent words and there is the spoken word. In all three forms words are powerful, but it is the spoken word that shakes things up the most. It is by the power of the spoken word that I can reach into the invisible realm. Consider this: When you pray, as you speak into the spiritual realm, a whisper can be heard halfway around the world. Not only can it be heard, when it is spoken under the influence of the Holy Spirit, it can change things!

As you begin to examine the spiritual armor, you will discover that each piece is symbolic of the spoken word. Do not forget! It is not our word that constitutes God's mighty armor. It is God's word in our mouth!

Let's take a look at two events in Jesus' ministry that reinforce this truth.

Matthew 8: 5 When Jesus had entered Capernaum, a centurion came to him, asking for help. 6 "Lord," he said, "my servant lies at home paralyzed and in terrible suffering." 7 Jesus said to him, "I will go and heal him." 8 The centurion replied, "Lord, I do not deserve to have You come under my roof. But just say the word, and my servant will be healed. 9 For I myself am a man under authority, with soldiers under me. I tell this one, 'Go,' and he goes; and that one, 'Come,' and he comes. I say to my servant, 'Do this,' and he does it." 10 When Jesus heard this, He was astonished and said to those following Him, "I tell you the truth, I have not found anyone in Israel with such great faith. 11 I say to you that many will come from the east and the west, and will take their places at the feast with Abraham, Isaac and Jacob in the kingdom of heaven. 12 But the subjects of the kingdom will be thrown outside, into the darkness, where there will be weeping and gnashing of teeth." 13 Then Jesus said to the centurion, "Go! It will be done just as you believed it would." And his servant was healed at that very hour. (NIV)

There are three key elements in this story, faith, authority and the spoken word. It takes all three to be an effective spiritual warrior. It is no mystery that this Roman Soldier had reached such a great level of success. He had achieved a high rank in an army filled with ambitious men. He had won the favor of many in Rome, but more amazing, he had won the favor of the Jews under his authority. One of the reasons for this fact was that he had not abused his authority. When he said, "I am a man under authority." he was demonstrating the rightful respect for the authority that had been given him. He understood why people did what he told them to do. He had faith that Rome would back him, because he was under Roman authority. Without the Roman government no one would be compelled to listen to him. He had knowledge of Rome's mandate. He had a clear understanding of his rank and position with Rome and he had absolute faith that Rome would back his commands as long as he was a man under authority.

This man did not achieve his status and the level of success he had in a weekend seminar. He did not develop the discipline required for this kind of life casually. His lifestyle was not developed by setting aside 45 minutes every Sunday and attending a few special events here and there. This man acknowledged what authority he was under and what authority that gave him in every event of his life. He was not putting on a show for Jesus when he made this statement of faith. It was as natural as breathing for him. It was his way of life. He didn't muster this up at the bedside of his servant. By the time his servant fell ill, this Soldier's faith was already intact. Too often you try to put on the armor at the point of need. At this point it is too late. It is like trying to learn how to swim only after you are tossed into the water. If you are to prevail at this point it will be because another warrior stepped in on your behalf.

Simply speak the word! You too have the ability to have such power. Like this Roman Soldier you must be a person under authority. You must be under the authority of God, by the power of His Holy Spirit. By the Holy Spirit, you must know what God's will is for this battle. When you have revelation knowledge of God's will, faith will come. When faith comes, you will have the courage to speak boldly and you will see the power of God move in a powerful way. People fail to speak out loud in matters of spiritual warfare because they have failed in one or more of the three key elements which are faith, authority and the spoken word. Without this you are not ready for battle.

Luke 4:1 Jesus, full of the Holy Spirit, returned from the Jordan and was led by the Spirit in the desert, 2 where for forty days He was tempted by the devil. He ate nothing during those days, and at the end of them He was hungry. 3 The devil said to Him, "If You are the Son of God, tell this stone to become bread." 4 Jesus answered, "It is written: 'Man does not live on bread alone.' " 5 The devil led Him up to a high place and showed Him in an instant all the kingdoms of the world. 6 And he said to Him, "I will give You all their authority and splendor, for it has been given to me, and I can give it to anyone I want to. 7 So if You worship me, it will all be Yours." 8 Jesus answered, "It is written: 'Worship the Lord your God and serve Him only.' " 9 The devil led Him to Jerusalem and had Him stand on the highest point of the temple. "If you are the Son of God," he said, "throw Yourself down from here. 10 For it is written:" 'He will command His angels concerning You to guard You carefully; 11 they will lift You up in their hands, so that You will not strike Your foot against a stone.' " 12 Jesus answered, "It says: 'Do not put the Lord your God to the test.' " 13 When the devil had finished all this tempting, he left Him until an opportune time. (NIV)

In this passage we see the same three elements in play. As Satan attacked Jesus with these temptations, Jesus won the battle because He knew what authority He was under. He had absolute faith in that authority and this faith caused Him to speak. When he spoke He spoke the words of God.

People often fail in time of temptation, because they never speak. It has been said by many people over the years, that "the battlefield is in the mind." I believe this is true. With the mind being the battlefield, then it is a war of thoughts. The loudest thought decides the outcome of the battle! A word on a page is more powerful when it is spoken out loud! During the battle, the spoken word is your advantage. Thoughts are more powerful when they are spoken. Satan can produce thoughts all day long, but because he lacks a physical body, he cannot speak a word.

With this truth in mind go back to the conflict with the co-worker mentioned in the beginning of this book. These questions arise: "What would Jesus say?" "What is God's thought on this situation?" Though this scenario is incomplete, most likely, additional detail would be unnecessary. With the limited picture one might find Isaiah 54:17 useful.

Isaiah 64:17 "But in that coming day, no weapon turned against you will succeed. And everyone who tells lies in court will be brought to justice. These benefits are enjoyed by the servants of the LORD; their vindication will come from me. I, the LORD, have spoken!"

Remember, the written word is powerful, but the spoken word is more powerful. Before you majestically bark out this verse, remember the three key elements: authority, faith and the spoken word. From this truth I might say, out loud, "What this person has said about me is untrue. It was designed to hurt me, but it will not work because my God says He will vindicate me! God, I thank You and I trust You to do what You have said!"

With this statement I have demonstrated the symbolism of the "belt of truth," "the breastplate of righteousness" and the "sword of the Spirit."

5. Stay on the offence.

It is often said that the best offense is a good defense. While this may be true in sports, it is never true in war. If you are in a defensive position in a war, it means your enemy has, for the moment, gotten the advantage over you. In all eternity, God has never been in a defensive position.

Consider the story of Joseph. If you are not familiar with this story, or if time has passed since you last read it, you might want to take a moment and read it. You will find this story in Genesis Chapter 37 through Genesis Chapter 48. From the well to slavery and then to prison, Joseph trusted God. He responded to each crisis in his life with character and faith. In the natural it looked as though Joseph would surely die in jail. Throughout the first part of his life it seemed things were hopelessly messed up. When we read the story from start to finish, we see God's master plan for Joseph's life. I do not believe that God planned for Joseph to be thrown in the well nor sold into slavery. Those were sinful acts of hateful men. The beauty of the story is that regardless of what other people did to Joseph they could not interrupt God's plan for this man. God never played defense. God never had to stop and adjust His plan. God swiftly and with purpose moved Joseph to the place He intended.

There is a key lesson illustrated in the life of Joseph. Joseph was not a reactive person. That is to say, his actions were not driven by external causes. Joseph was a responsive person. This means when external things happened Joseph's action was driven from within.

My wife and I like to watch the television program called "Untold Stories of the Emergency Room." Watching doctors and nurses work in the emergency room vividly demonstrates the difference between reacting and responding. As they deal with emergencies, their responses are based on their vast training. Often family and friends are there as their loved ones are brought to the emergency room with life threatening injuries and illnesses. They are terrified and often very emotional as they react to the emergency. The doctor remains calm. If the doctor lets his or her emotions drive their actions they will be unable to attend to the emergency effectively. The response to the emergency is based on their knowledge and training.

With this in mind, consider the following chart.

EMERGENCY
Crisis Situation
Battle

React - Defense		Respond - Offense
Instant - Reflex	-	Thought out
Instinctive - Carnal	-	Disciplined - Spiritual
Emotion Based	-	Values Based
Short-term Consideration	-	Long-term Consideration
Easy Way Out - Quick Fix	-	Honorable Way Out
Accepts Terms & Conditions	-	Sets Terms & Conditions
Unprepared - Surprised	-	Prepared - Expects to win
Surrenders or Compromises	-	Conquers

The one line that I wish to highlight in the previous chart deals with the terms and conditions. Think back to the battle between David and Goliath. Twice a day for forty days, Goliath stepped out into clear view of King Saul and the armies of Israel. Each time he challenged them to a contest. He would represent the Philistines as their champion and would fight whomever Israel chose for their champion. One of the terms Goliath offered was a "winner-take-all" event. The idea was that only one soldier would die. There were two major problems with this plan. First, the Philistines had unlawfully invaded Israel. "What sense would it make to make a lawful agreement with an army whose very presence demonstrated their lawlessness?" "What assurance or expectation would there be that they would abide by the terms they had proposed?" The second problem is the biggest one. For forty days, Israel allowed their enemy to set the terms and conditions of the battle. If I were to face off with someone in a contest, I would choose a contest that favored my set of skills. I have a friend named Randy Mayes. He is three or four years older than I am. He is in good physical condition and runs in marathons. I am 50 lbs overweight and have never been a good runner. If I were going to challenge Randy to a contest, I would not choose running. I think I might challenge him to a spirited game of chess. Chess is a hobby of mine and I am fairly good at it. The point is that King Saul, for some unexplainable reason, felt the need to accept the terms and conditions of his enemy. Saul had a seasoned army. A careful examination of the full passage of Scripture tells us that, after Goliath lost his head, the armies of Israel routed the Philistines. This fact, combined with the proposal Goliath offered, leads me to believe that, without Goliath, the Philistines were at a disadvantage. After all, they were on foreign soil. They were only about eight miles from Jerusalem. This fact would favor the Israelites whenever they needed supplies. The Philistines had chosen their strongest advantage and convinced Israel to accept the terms and conditions for the fight. I believe that Saul could have summoned his army. He could have explained to them that the Philistines are hiding behind one man and even though this man was a giant, he was still only one man. On day one, as Goliath came out the second time to hurl insults at Israel and their God, the mighty host of Israel could have set their terms and conditions as they stormed the camp of the Philistines. It might have taken ten or twelve men to bring down mighty Goliath. It could even have taken less! What ever the case, history tells us that when Goliath died, so also did the heart of the Philistines. King Saul reacted and allowed his enemy to set the terms of battle until a teenage boy came along and said, by his actions, "I have some terms of my own to set." Read for yourself and see how David redefined the terms of the battle. He defined the terms based on his strength. He did not consent to the terms nor to the conditions set by his enemy.

1 Samuel 17: 45 "David shouted in reply, 'You come to me with sword, spear, and javelin, but I come to you in the name of the LORD Almighty -- the God of the armies of Israel, whom you have defied. 46 Today the LORD will conquer you, and I will kill you and cut off your head. And then I will give the dead bodies of your men to the birds and wild animals, and the whole world will know that there is a God in Israel! 47 And everyone will know that the LORD does not need weapons to rescue his people. It is his battle, not ours. The LORD will give you to us!'"

When our spiritual enemy comes to you, he will attempt to get you to fight in the arena of emotions. He will attempt to make the battle all about you, and not about the Kingdom of God. He knows the only chance he has to prevail against you is to separate you from our Champion, Jesus. When confronted with a battle don't rush in. Take some time to pray and seek God. Get your Bible out and prepare your battle plan. Don't react instinctively. There is not true power there. Respond with the supernatural power of God.

CHAPTER FIVE

THE BELT OF TRUTH

John 17:17 Thy word is truth.

In Ephesians 6, Paul uses the belt to symbolize truth. In the suite of armor, the belt served three significant purposes. Clothing in that day was much different than that which is worn today. It was often baggy and could easily get in the way. Zippers and buttons did not exist. The belt was an important item. The most obvious function of the belt was to hold the pants up! This may sound a little funny, but imagine a fight between two great warriors. If one of them is struggling to keep his pants up, he will be distracted and insecure in the fight. The belt of truth keeps him from being embarrassed or ashamed in battle. It keeps him covered.

The belt also served as a place to hang things, such as the sword. Today the term "tool belt" is a common phrase. The armor that Paul wrote about, the sword and other items of importance were attached to the belt. Look at a police officer's belt some time. Without his belt, he would not be able to manage all the items which are necessary for his job. Imagine Clint Eastwood or John Wayne in one of the many Western movies in which they played. The characters they portrayed proudly wore their gun belts. True to history, many of these Western warriors would carve notches on their belts to signify their victories.

In most societies throughout history, the belt was used as a symbol of the warriors' success. A gunfighter would often carve a clearly visible notch in his belt to signify his victories. In most forms of martial arts, the person's level is indicated by the color of his belt. Fighters send a powerful message by the color the belt they wear. A black belt is feared, even when nothing is known about the person who wears it. In a boxing match, the champion has a belt. He took the belt from the previous champion when he defeated him. The belt is symbolic. It says that the person, who possesses this belt, is the champion. It tells those, who are not confident in their skill, to be afraid. Few will have any desire to challenge and even fewer have the ability to prevail. From the earliest records of history we see the belt used to symbolize the victories. We do not have to enter spiritual battles with our belt. God gives us His belt! He is undefeated in all of history. The demons of Hell know this belt well and the fear it greatly!

When we strap on the belt of truth, we send a message to our enemy from far off. Some will flee at the very sight of a saint, well versed in the truth. Others will choose to fight, but they know the power of the truth, because they have been conquered by its power many times before. Demons know better than anyone the power of truth! A lie has never, not even one time, prevailed against the truth. Lies only prevail against ignorance or apathy.

Knowing the truth has no value by itself. I have heard people say, "If you know the truth, the truth will set you free." This is not true. James 2:19 tells us, "even the demons know there is a God." The demons often cried out to Jesus, demonstrating that they knew the truth of who He was, but there was no redemption in simply knowing. Let's look at this scripture in context and see what it really says about truth.

John 8: 31 "To the Jews who had believed Him, Jesus said, 'If you hold to My teaching, you are really My disciples. 32 Then you will know the truth, and the truth will set you free.'"

First, notice that Jesus is speaking to Jews who had believed in Him. I believe from this, we could refer to these people as "believers." Each Sunday our church pews are filled with believers. Being a true believer is the entry level into the kingdom. The next step is critical if you are going to live the life promised to every child of God. The next step is being a disciple. To be a disciple you must hold to the teachings of Jesus. In John 1, Jesus is called The Word. The whole of the Bible was inspired by His Holy Spirit. The King James version of the Bible says, "if you continue in My word." This means that you live there. If you are dedicated to the teaching of Jesus, then the next step occurs. You will know the truth!

I have a friend named Kelly Anderson. Kelly knows racing! He has been involved in sprint car racing for many years. A few years ago, Kelly began taking me to the races and teaching me the "ins" and "outs" of the sport. Today I know about sprint car racing, but Kelly knows sprint car racing. He can take a car apart down to the frame and put it back together. He can listen to the pitch of the engine and know things about it that I will never understand. He knows the right tire pressure for each tire and how to adjust that pressure for different track conditions. Kelly knows sprint cars. I only know "about" sprint cars. If I decided, with the knowledge I have about this sport, to get my own car, set it up and race it, chances are high that I would hurt others and myself. In Acts 19, there is a story that demonstrates the difference between knowing the truth and knowing about the truth. Seven sons of Sceva were attempting to deliver a demon-possessed man. They said. "I command you by Jesus, whom Paul preaches, to come out!" The demon replied, "I know Jesus and I know Paul, but who are you?" The sons of Sceva were then attacked and escaped naked and injured. These men knew about the truth, but they were not intimate with the truth. The word Jesus used when He said, "You will know the truth…" was a Jewish idiom for sexual intercourse between a man and a woman, to become acquainted with, or know. These men knew about the truth, but they were not intimate with it. My friend Kelly is intimate with sprint car racing. This simply means he is very close to it. It is dear to his heart.

There is no short cut to this level of intimacy with the truth. To know the truth requires discipleship. Discipleship requires a dedication to the Word of God. When you follow the simple instruction Jesus gave in John 8: 31-32, the result will be freedom! It is a worthwhile endeavor!

This would be the shortest chapter in the book if people understood what truth is. Cultures and societies worldwide struggle with the concept of truth. One concept that is prevalent in the world today. It is called "relativism." It is pounded into our children from the first day of school. It is a central theme in most colleges throughout the world. It is in our secular music and present in every form of modern media. It has saturated the "baby-boom" generation and all those who are younger. It is steadily creeping into the older generations as well. A simple way to sum up "relativism" is this; "What's true for you isn't necessarily true for me and what's true for me may not be true for you." Another way of saying it is this: "There is no absolute truth." You will hear the success of this indoctrination when you listen to a group of teenagers discuss an issue. Often you will hear someone say, "Well, for me, what this means…" People, who preface a statement this way, have been trained not to offend someone else who may believe differently. They have been taught that what is true for them, may not be true for others. A question you will hear people ask is, "Who are you to say what is right or wrong?" This question is another challenge to the concept of absolute truth.

My favorite way to begin a discussion with someone who believes this way is to establish that they do, in fact, believe there is no absolute truth. Once we have established their belief, I then ask, "Is that absolutely true?" This points out the paradox of relativism. From there I go on to point out a number of absolute truths. Physics and math both demonstrate absolute truth. Somewhere in the discussion, moral relativism will come up. This deception is more difficult to deal with. If you have begun this way of thinking, you will face a world of many tests and no answers. Jesus said it plainly in John 17:17. Thy Word is truth.

Cultural Relativism vs. the Truth

Alex sat quietly at his desk. As he stared hopelessly at the test paper in front of him, he considered the way he had prepared for this test. Math had always been a challenging subject for him, but he had entered the classroom today, confident that he was ready, but now, nearly 30 minutes had passed and he could only answer three or four of the 25 questions with any degree of confidence. As he looked over each question for the fifth or sixth time, one phrase was repeated over and over in his head. "I don't know!" Alex felt panic, as tears of anxiety welled up in his eyes. To cry in high school, there, in front of his peers, would only make matters worse.

One of the most stressful things in life is to be confronted by a test of any kind without the correct answer. It is overwhelming to be asked an important question and have to respond, "I don't know." This response often precedes failure. Hosea 4:6 says, "My people are destroyed for lack of knowledge." Imagine for a moment being confronted with important questions several times a day and always having to answer them, "I don't know." Take a moment and imagine the destructive impact this ignorance has on a person's self image. This is kind of the world that many people live in today. It is a world that has been created by a false doctrine known as "cultural relativism." This doctrine is pounded into our kids on a daily basis in our public schools and by every modern media. While the impact of this false doctrine is evident in our youth, it has, in fact, permeated every age group. I have heard senior citizens say things like, "Who are we to say that lifestyle is wrong?" Cultural Relativism can easily excuse the immoral acts of celebrities and politicians. As they are given one free pass after another, our own consciousness is numbed as we make excuses instead of confronting immoral behavior.

Relativism says there is no absolute truth. Cultural Relativism is a little more detailed. Cultural relativism is the view that all ethical truth is relative to a specified culture. According to cultural relativism, it is never true to say that a certain kind of behavior is right or wrong. Cultural Relativism says what is true for you may not be true for me. If there is no absolute truth, then there can be no absolute right or wrong. If there is no absolute right or wrong, then, when times of testing come into our lives, the answer will always be, "I don't know." If you are to have any hope of winning in the battles in this day of war, you must know the absolute truth. People, who make adjustments to the truth in order to accommodate their culture, are weak and susceptible to deceit. It is possible for these people to completely agree with the Bible, but yet immediately dismiss it as not relative to them in their life. It may be true for you and work in your life, but in my life I choose to adopt a different truth. Cultural Relativism is fine and dandy until a test comes along. Tests require absolute answers. I believe that the epidemic of depression and anxiety in society today is a direct result of constantly being confronted with questions that require an answer based on absolute truth and having to say, "I don't know." How far can I go with my girlfriend? Should I go to a party where they are smoking weed? Is oral sex really sex? Does life really begin at conception? Relativism leaves its victim in the dark on every important moral question. There is no absolute truth. Therefore, there can be no right or wrong. The answer to all life's major questions is, "I don't know."

Consider the research of Josh McDowell and George Barna. Their research shows that 63 % of youth, who actively attend church believe that

Muslims, Buddhists, Christians and Jews all pray to the same god; they just use different names. When it comes to Jesus, 87% believe that He was a real person; 78% believe that He was born of a virgin. Before I began to deal with this issue, I would have assumed that all the kids in my youth group were exceptions to these findings. I would have assumed that the number in my youth group to be 100%. I am not so naive today. I found that, in line with Josh McDowell's numbers, a large number of kids in our youth group believed that Jesus committed sin. I also found that over half of the kids in my youth group believed that, if you were really committed to your religion, you would go to heaven, regardless of what religion it was. A person who thinks this way can sit in our church services today and agree with everything that is said and still miss the truth. They hear what we say as a truth, but it is only one of many truths! When the battle comes into their lives, they have no support. Without the belt of truth, they struggle with confidence. Unable to define good and evil, they will be exposed to one failure after another.

Until you are grounded in the absolute, unshakeable and unchanging truth, that is God's Word, you will not prevail in spiritual battles. I encourage you to study and learn all you can about apologetics. Ground yourself in the knowledge that what God says is absolutely true all the time. Then search for what God has to say about everything in your life.

Satan has waged war on the truth because it is damning to him. One of his major handicaps is that he doesn't understand the truth. The Bible says that his only language is lies. (John 8:44 and Romans 8:31-38) Let's go back to the example of my friend Kelly and I and our respective knowledge of sprint car racing. I know about sprint car racing, but I do not have a working knowledge of it. I lack understanding. When I am in the pits with Kelly, I can listen as he and the pit crew discuss the race, but I do not understand what they are saying. If I had my own race team, perhaps I could spy on Kelly's crew and listen to all they had to say about the race, but it still would remain meaningless to me. In the same way, when believers begin to speak the truth about certain things, Satan is out of the loop. He and his demons are unable to understand what is being talked about. This fact seals his fate every time and gives us an unbeatable advantage over our enemy!

Facts & Truth

On August 18, 1985, Kristin Nicole Porter was born. (My daughter) She was nine weeks early. Initially things looked good, but on day three, an infection developed in her kidneys. I will never forget listening to the doctor explain the facts of her condition to us. This doctor was an atheist. Lisa, my wife and I were devout believers. What the facts told her and what they told us were different. The facts told her that our daughter only had a 60% chance to live. The facts meant that Kristin would be in intensive care for up to five months, if she lived. The facts told all of us that this was a very serious circumstance. As this doctor went through all the biological facts, my mind raced through the scriptures I knew. One of the first steps I took upon hearing the news was based on Matthew 18; 19-20. Lisa was still recovering from a caesarean section. Needless to say she was not well. We prayed before I left her to rest and recover. My first phone call was to a close spiritual friend. He arranged to leave work early and we met at his home. This was the beginning of a spiritual conflict. We laid the facts out before God and prayed. We looked to God to see what He would say about these facts, knowing that what God says is true! When He showed us what His Will for this circumstance was, we activated it by speaking it, OUT LOUD! Five weeks later our beautiful baby came home! She is alive and healthy today in spite of the facts, because of the power of knowing and speaking the truth!

Genuine facts do not contradict the truth. However, if we are not intimate with the truth, facts can mislead us. If this happens, we will draw the wrong conclusions and believe the wrong things. The faith we need is only accessible through the truth. All facts are subject to the truth. Facts are nothing more than information. Information is very important in war, but it is faith that will win. It is important to base your faith on the truth and not on the facts. Facts will often change, but truth never has and never will change. It was a fact that Kristin had a life-threatening illness. The truth was, and forever will be: "There is healing in the name of Jesus!"

Consider the contrast between facts and truth in light of the battle between David and Goliath. The Bible spells out all the facts. The size of the giant and all of his weapons and the size of David and his tiny sling are all laid out clearly. You will find this event recorded in 1 Samuel 17.

Based on facts alone, anyone would expect the giant to win, but David knew the truth!

Truth can have a powerful impact on the facts. Facts will never impact the truth.

In the months preceding Kristin's birth, I had been driving eight to nine hours a day. While I was driving, I listened to Kenneth Copeland sermons and other teaching tapes. Several hours every day, five days a week, I listened to the preaching of God's Word. This created a hunger that would drive me to my Bible whenever I got the chance. It was not some heavy duty religious act, which I felt obligated to do. It was an exciting journey of faith. I was experiencing more freedom than I ever imagined. I didn't do it because I feared an upcoming struggle. I was doing it because I loved Jesus. Even though I was not looking for the battle, one was surely on its way.

A dominate part of Kenneth Copeland's teaching is on healing. When the battle erupted, I did not run out to the nearest Christian book store and buy three or four books on God's healing power. I had devoted myself to teachings of Jesus. Therefore, I knew the truth and the truth set us free! If you should find yourself in a battle and you have not devoted yourself to God's Word, find someone who has and get him or her to help you. If you are not in a battle now, get ready! Soon enough you will need the armor. You will face a circumstance that will require spiritual strength. It is better to acquire your black belt in the gym, than to learn while you are on the battlefield.

Remember, we live in a day of war. Our enemy has tricks and strategies. In the days, months and years ahead of you, he will attack you with illness, divorces, financial ruin, depression, fear and countless other plagues. For him, this is not a game. It's all-out war. He has not overlooked you. When you engage him or any of his cohorts, if you have on the sturdy belt of truth, they will see it. From a distance, you will instill fear, some will flee without a fight. You may not even know they were present. Others will fight, but their confidence from the first moment of the battle will be shaken. This will reduce the duration of the battle. In the end you will always prevail, with the sturdy belt of truth!

Finally, don't forget why we "put on the armor!" Jesus said the gates of hell would not prevail against us. We are not fighting a defensive fight for selfish reasons. We are fighting an offensive mission to advance the kingdom of God. We are fighting an offensive battle to win souls.

The fight for my newborn daughter's life began as a defensive struggle, but the moment Lisa and I turned to Jesus, He turned things around. Each day Kristin thrived in that intensive care unit was a blow against the atheist belief system the neonatologist. This neonatologist had been harsh with many believers who worked under her. What God did in Kristin's body turned the doctor's facts upside-down. It encouraged the believers in that intensive care unit. It encouraged other parents who had children in there. It has been a wonderful testimony for many years. By God's grace, this fight has been an offensive fight that continues to advance His kingdom to this day.

Chapter Six

The Breastplate of Righteousness

Isaiah 54:17 "'No weapon that is formed against thee shall prosper; and every tongue that shall rise against thee in judgment thou shalt condemn. This is the heritage of the servants of the LORD, and their righteousness is of me,' saith the LORD."

One of my favorite movies of all time is Braveheart. Towards the end of the movie, there is one of the most powerful scenes I have ever watched in a movie. The main character, William Wallace, is the feared warrior. He fought with a reckless abandon. He fought with heart! In this scene his army has been badly beaten. One of the reasons they had suffered loss was that he was betrayed by leaders within his ranks. Perhaps, as a last act of defiance, Wallace gave chase to the opposing king and his men. In response the king dispatches one of his men. You cannot see the face of the man he dispatches because he is wearing a helmet. As the dispatched man engages Wallace, he is knocked from his horse. Wallace quickly gains the upper hand and is about to end the life of this soldier, when the helmet is ripped from his head. To Wallace's great surprise it is his trusted friend, who has betrayed him. In an instant all the fierceness is gone. Wallace releases this traitor, drops his weapon, slowly lies back on the ground, and waits to be killed. Of course, Wallace lives to fight another day. However, this scene graphically shows what it is to fight with heart and what it means to lose heart.

Every year I watch the Super Bowl. For my friends, who prefer soccer, this illustration will apply exactly in the same manner. However, while many of the recent Super Bowl games have been close, most championship games have been lopsided. One of my favorite Super Bowl games was between Tony Dungy of the Indianapolis Colts and Lovie Smith of the Chicago Bears. This game pitted two Christian coaches against each other. It was a classic match up. Both teams took the field expecting to win. The Bears opened by returning the kickoff for a touchdown! The Bears were underdogs in this contest, but with this break every player on the Bears team believed they had a chance to win. Midway thoughout the fourth quarter, the Bears found themselves down by a score of 29 to 17. As the final minutes of the game unfolded, you could see the Bears lose heart. The same players that only minutes before passed the side line and closely watched all the action on the field, sat on the bench, some with towels over their heads. They had lost heart.

In the battle between David and Goliath, we see a contest of a skilled warrior against a warrior with heart! This is not to say that David did not have skill. He was deadly with a sling. But what made this young boy a true warrior was heart!

Proverbs 4:23 says to guard your heart, for it affects everything you do. NLT.

There are two root causes that will lead to the loss of heart.

1. Fear! I am not able to win this battle.
2. Apathy. I do not care about the outcome of this battle.

For forty days Goliath mocked the fighting men of Israel. Not one man out of the thousands had the heart to face Goliath. Each day Goliath mocked them and the God of Israel . Not one man had the courage to stand and fight. A prolonged season of fear will often lead to apathy. We tell ourselves the battle is not important enough to try and cope with our resignation, that we have lost the fight. You can see this played out in politics. Many times in an election, when people are convinced their candidate has lost, they will stay home. Fear of loss leads to apathy and the person gives up without even being heard.

You might say of this person, "He has lost heart." Have you understood the meaning of the word I am emphasizing yet? The word is "heart!" In any contest, the person who loses heart will fail. Satan knows this. Remember, Satan and his demons are spirit beings. They can only reach into the physical realm, where we live, with the help of human beings. This takes us back to the battlefield of the mind. Simply put, the only weapon our enemy has is the lie. This weapon does the most damage if the enemy can get it into your heart. The Breastplate of Righteousness covers your heart. Not one of Satan's lies will ever pierce The Breastplate of Righteousness. Knowing this fact, Satan has worked through the ages to create a false concept, one, which has been taught in many churches for centuries. He has disguised this concept as humility. When a child of God accepts this false notion of humility, he or she will believe in being unworthy of The Breastplate of Righteousness and will refuse it. In doing so they believe they are being humble. These lowly souls will limp through life, never experiencing their birthright! This false humility often sounds like this. "I am just a sinner, saved by grace." I have heard this statement hundreds of times in my life. It is in songs and sermons. It laces the testimony of thousands of saints, but it is not true! The truth is, I was a sinner. However, when I was saved by grace, 2 Corinthians 5:17 says, "Old things are passed away." It says, we are new creatures. I used to be a sinner, but when Jesus came into my life, He killed the old man. I died with Christ and was raised a new creature! In Romans Chapter 7, Paul tells us that, even in his own life, he still struggles with his sinful flesh, but in Romans Chapter 8 he goes on to tell us that there is no condemnation because of the law of the Spirit of Life has set me free from the law of sin and death. When God looks at me, He sees His child. When He looks at me, He looks through the covenant blood of Jesus. He sees an heir! (Romans 8:17) This puts us in line for Isaiah 54:17 where God declares that our heritage is this: "Their righteousness is of me," saith the Lord. Do you remember what truth is? John 17:17 says, "Thy Word is truth." If God has said of me or you, that we are righteous, then it is settled. Be mindful of this truth. He only says this truth about His own. Jesus said that no one comes to the Father except through him. It is not of my own doing. It is the miracle of God's grace and mercy. By this amazing gift, purchased with such a great price, I can become a child of The Most High God. As a child and an heir, I have every right to put on the "breastplate of righteousness." When the devil comes to tell me about my mistakes, I plead the blood which has cleansed me of all unrighteousness. 2 Peter 1: 3-11 is good reading to reinforce this truth.

Having touched on humility and the false premise the devil has sold to many Christians, let's look at true biblical humility. Imagine a baseball player who always strikes out. The only time he ever gets on base is when he is "walked." He can't catch a simple pop fly and when he throws a ball, no one knows where it is going. Now imagine this player telling someone what a humble player he is. The truth is, he is a terrible player. He is not humble. To be humble he would need to have some degree of skill. A weak person is not humble. They are just weak. The higher the skill level the greater a person's ability to demonstrate humility. The simplest way I know to define the biblical kind of humility is "not being to impressed with yourself."

Humility is required to wear God's breastplate of Righteousness. After all, you are not strapping on your own breastplate. God will not give His breastplate to anyone who is not humble. 1 Peter 5:5 tells us that God resists the proud, but gives grace to the humble.

Righteousness simply means that I am in right standing with God. This is made possible by the shed blood of Jesus. My best effort is nothing more than filthy rags to God. Nothing I can do will move me even a tiny bit closer to right standing. My right-standing with God is based solely on what Jesus did.

Having already put on the sturdy belt of truth, I can now accept this breastplate as the Holy Spirit Himself straps it on for me! No lie can pierce it and no force on earth can remove it from me. As long as I am girded with the belt of truth, no devil can trick me into removing it. By God's grace, I am well on my way to being an effective spiritual warrior.

Chapter Seven

The shoes of peace

Psalms 37:37 "Look at those who are honest and good, for a wonderful future lies before those who love peace."

When I first preached on the message written in this book, God opened my eyes to something new every week. Note, I am not implying that there was anything new, just that it was new to me. By the time I got to the shoes of peace a sense of excitement had developed as God revealed more truth about spiritual warfare. I couldn't wait to finally get to the sword! Swords are cool and I was anxious to find out what God was going to show me about it! When it came to the week when I was to preach on the shoes of peace I was less than excited. How would I preach an entire sermon on shoes. I thought, perhaps I could combine it with something else and spice it up a little. With all this talk of war, it seemed to me that shoes of peace just didn't quite fit. What in the world could be exciting about shoes? Wow! Was I ever wrong! As I settled into the study and opened myself to God on this issue, He thrilled my soul with the revelation of the shoes of peace!

Growing up in southern Missouri, I lived in the country. My Grandpa Messenger owned a large dairy farm and I had access to all types of guns. I loved to hunt. I hunted mostly squirrels and rabbits. In 2002, my family and I moved to a small town in northern Iowa to pastor Calvary Gospel Assembly. In the fall of 2003, Greg McDonald, a member of that church and a good friend, invited me to go pheasant hunting. I had a nice 12 gauge shotgun and was thrilled at the invitation. I had observed the proper attire for pheasant hunting and did my best to dress accordingly. I went to the shoe closet and pulled out my hiking boots. They looked very much like the hunting boots my friend wore. I discovered two things that day. As we were on our way to the first field where we would hunt, I discovered egg coffee. Egg coffee is delightful! If you are curious about the egg coffee, I have one word for you, "Google." The second thing I learned that day is that there is a profound difference between hiking boots and the hunting boots my friend wore. Kicking through the waste high prairie grass was far different than the terrain I had experienced as a boy hunting rabbits. The heavy hiking boots burned energy and strained muscles with every step. I did not notice at first, but by early afternoon, my legs were burning. By the end of the day I could no longer keep up with my friend. This experience coincided with my sermon about the shoes of peace. I was still sore and walking strangely the Sunday I preached on the shoes of peace.

Most of us have a few pairs of shoes. When my daughter moved out on her own, I was shocked at how many boxes of shoes she had. Shoes denote where we are going. If I put on my house slippers, I am going to the couch to watch a little television or to read. If I put on my dress shoes, I am going to the office or church. If I grab my grass-stained tennis shoes, I am heading out to do yard work. There are more options, but you get the picture. Shoes forecast where I intend to go.

One Sunday morning I discovered that dress shoes should not be worn when riding my motorcycle. Often intersections have tiny loose gravel all over the pavement. My slick lightweight dress shoes slipped as I tried to establish my footing. I was able to keep my bike upright, but I discovered that I was unprepared for the road conditions with the shoes that I had chosen. When choosing the right shoes, you need to look ahead. It takes preparation to make sure we have on the right kind of footwear. Most of us know what it is like to have the wrong shoes for the occasion. Having the right footwear requires us to look at weather forecasts or to consider what we will be doing later. In the case of armor, our forecast is peace. Our expectation is to do what needs to be done to bring the peace of God.

The symbolism of shoes where peace is concerned is as rich as any symbolism in this passage. It gives us the idea of being well-grounded or having a good foundation.

Let's go back to the hypothetical scenario from chapter one. Remember the co-worker and his conflict. In this scenario we emphasized that we wrestle not with flesh and blood. We established the truth; that this is a spiritual battle. Think about this conflict. What is the goal of the natural person? There are many selfish motives, which could be the foundation of the conflict. Such as: revenge, dominance, or political gain. Your desired goal going into the conflict will not only shape the battle, it will shape your personality. Victory is the worst thing that could happen to you if your motivation is wrong. Victory will reward and reinforce your behavior. Take a minute and reflect on the following statements.

- I fight because I enjoy the thrill of winning.
- I fight because I hate the way things are going.
- I fight because I want things to go my way.
- I fight because I am angry. Enough is enough!
- I fight because I must, to end evil and establish peace.

Which statement will bring about the most desirable outcome in the conflict with the co-worker?

When peace is not the warrior's motive, each battle will harden them a little more. Win or lose, one battle at a time, they lose their tenderness. They will reach a point that when peace is an option, they will choose to continue fighting. Through the ages, there have been many warriors who have suffered this fate. When the war ended, they were lost. They felt they had no purpose. Their hardened hearts felt the need for war and conflict. They did not know how to enjoy peace. This will not be your fate if you put on the shoes of peace. Your motives and intentions will be grounded in peace in each phase of the battle.

Consider the outcome of the co-worker conflict. Should you gain the upper hand with the wrong motive, your behavior will provoke her even more. Often it will pull others into the conflict as it grows like a tumor. The temporary victory will spur on other conflicts in an endless attempt to satisfy selfish concerns.

A spirit-led warrior will never fight because of hatred. They fight because they love. When we celebrate, we do not rejoice over the crushed opponent. We celebrate the advance of the Kingdom of Jesus. One thousand years from today, we will not be celebrating the defeat of the devil. He will be long forgotten. We will celebrate the victory of King Jesus forever!

The warrior who loves and fights for peace will feel the thrill of victory. He or she will be stirred at times with anger and hatred of evil. These are all part of the battle, but you must guard your heart, so these emotions do not become your prime motivation. Your shoes of peace will serve as a constant reminder of your motive.

Having the correct footwear is a sign of preparation. If a person shows up wearing a pair of flip-flops to play basketball, it is evident that he did not think ahead. Remember, you live in a day of war. Conflicts of every kind await you at every turn. Many times you are taken by surprise when conflicts arise. Once the fight begins, it is too late to begin preparing. If you have not made the needed preparation before the battle begins, you will find yourself reacting instinctively. Peace is not a natural human instinct in a fight. It is the instinct of a dog to chase a car. It takes training and discipline to break this instinct. It is a human instinct to react to conflict with a self-centered outlook. To change this behavior it requires time in God's Word. A sermon once or twice a month and a devotional now and then will not equip you. Those selfish instincts are powerful. As an athlete prepares for his or her event or as a special operations soldier prepares for his mission, you must prepare to meet with events that will stir you carnal instincts.

As Jesus confronted the Pharisees, time and again during His ministry, He never lost sight of the fact that we wrestle not with flesh and blood. As they challenged Him, lied about Him, mocked Him, laid traps for Him and even tried to kill Him He never lost His temper. He responded to every challenge with the actions that were rooted in His readiness that comes from the gospel of peace.

In Philippians 4, Paul addresses a conflict between two of his co-workers in ministry. He encouraged them to settle their conflict. He also encouraged others to help bring about a peaceful end to their dispute. He gave a couple noteworthy instructions. He said to be considerate in all you do. Then he reminded them that the Lord is coming soon. The keys to a successful battle can be found in this section of Scripture. What Paul is saying here is to consider our actions in the light of the fact that Jesus is coming soon. This fact should shape the conflict. In some cases, consideration of the return of King Jesus will stop the conflict dead in its tracks. When a fight is unavoidable, our actions during the fight should be governed by the truth that Jesus is coming. This knowledge will bring joy to our battle and will establish Philippians 4:7 in our life.

Philippians 4:7 "If you do this, you will experience God's peace, which is far more wonderful than the human mind can understand. His peace will guard your hearts and minds as you live in Christ Jesus." (NLT)

Even in the midst of the fiercest battle we can know peace! It is a powerful testimony and a wonderful way to live in this day of war.

CHAPTER EIGHT

THE SHIELD OF FAITH

Psalms 3:3 "But You, O LORD, are a shield around me, my glory, and the One who lifts my head high."

At this point I want to take some time and reinforce the truth that all the armor explained in Ephesians 6 is symbolic. We read in Psalms that the Lord is our shield and in Ephesians, we see that faith is our shield. Do we have two shields to choose from? The answer is no. In fact, there is no shield. The shield is symbolic of the protection God provides to stifle the enemy's lies. The enemy's lies are symbolized as flaming arrows. Satan does not have literal flaming arrows. Every piece of armor is symbolic of God's Word. Every piece of armor works when we speak His Word! Too many warriors are silent today. It is time to speak God's Word. To do this, we must know God's Word. We must become students. King David spoke many times about his love for God's Word. He devoted his life to it. He did not do it out of obligation. It was not a religious practice. It was something he loved to do.

The symbols Paul chose in this passage paint a picture to help us understand things in the unseen world. Symbols are not effective if they are taken literally.

As we look at the shield of faith, it is important that we picture the shield that was in Paul's mind as he wrote. There are many kinds of shields. The come in all shapes and sizes. In history, some shields worked very well, whereas others were ineffective. Do a Google search on the "Armor of God" and you will see several examples of shields. Most of them are nothing like the shield that Paul envisioned as he wrote Ephesians 6.

To gain an understanding of what kind of shield Paul was talking about, we are going to take a look at the Greek word Paul used in Ephesians 6:16. The Greek word here is, "Thureos" (Phonetic thoo-reh-os'). The definition for this word is "a shield, a large oblong, four cornered shield." The word was taken from another Greek word, *Thura*, which simply means "door."

A *Thureos* shield was a specific shield. Paul was not speaking of a generic shield. The shield he spoke of here was large, like a door. A soldier could hide his entire body behind this shield.

The Roman legionaries in Paul's day carried this large shield. It provided more protection than other smaller shields, but made swift movement a little more difficult. The Thureos shield originally had an oval shape, but over time they curved the tops and sides to produce the type of shield which the Apostle Paul references in Ephesians 6. The Romans used their shields to create a tortoise-like formation called a *testudo* in which entire groups of soldiers would be enclosed in an armored box to provide protection against arrows. Many ancient shield designs featured incuts of one sort or another. These incuts were done to accommodate the shaft of a spear, thus facilitating tactics requiring the soldiers to stand close together forming a wall of shields.

Paul was talking about the kind of shield used by the Romans in his day. The Romans had developed a shield that was not just a defensive weapon. It allowed their army to advance against their enemies in a unique fashion. Wars are fought in phases. Many of us have followed the wars fought in Iraq and Afghanistan over the past two decades. These wars began with aerial assaults from war ship and planes. At some point the effectiveness of the ships and planes begin to drop. When the attack from the planes and war ships begins to lose effectiveness the infantry is called to move in on foot. In the day that the Apostle Paul lived, the battle would open with an assault from the archers. As they fired their arrows, the sky would grow dark. Often there would be so many arrows flying that the sun would be blocked out as though thick storms clouds had moved in. For centuries research and development increased the range of the arrow. The archers were deadly as long as they could keep their opponents far away. Once a skilled warrior with a sword got close to the archer, the long bow and arrow was no longer effective. In the day of the long bow, the key to winning a battle was to cross the kill zone. The kill zone was the area where the long bow and arrow were most effective.

Now, let's consider how this symbolism works in the spiritual war we are fighting. Satan and his demons are launching their flaming arrows. They are trying to keep us far away. The arrow is symbolic of lies. The flame is symbolic of how these lies spread if they are allowed to strike their target. With the shield of faith we can enter the kill zone. Our shields work best when we join together with other believers. When we join our faith with other Believers we can carefully work our way through the kill zone until we stand toe-to-toe with the archers. Then we pull out the Sword of the Spirit which is the Word of God and strike them down.

Matthew 18: 19 "I also tell you this: If two of you agree down here on earth concerning anything you ask, My Father in heaven will do it for you. 20 For where two or three gather together because they are Mine, I am there among them."

The one thing we must understand in order to pick up the shield of faith is, there is nothing selfish about biblical faith! For a better understanding of this statement, let us take a look at Hebrews Chapter 11.

Hebrews 11: 1 "Now faith is the substance of things hoped for, the evidence of things not seen. 2 For by it the elders obtained a good report. 3 Through faith we understand that the worlds were framed by the Word of God, so that things which are seen were not made of things which do appear. 4 By faith Abel offered unto God a more excellent sacrifice than Cain, by which he obtained witness that he was righteous, God testifying of his gifts: and by it he being dead yet speaketh. 5 By faith Enoch was translated that he should not see death; and was not found, because God had translated him: for before his translation he had this testimony, that he pleased God. 6 But without faith it is impossible to please him: for he that cometh to God must believe that He is, and that He is a rewarder of them that diligently seek Him." (KJV)

Look at verse four. By faith Able offered. Faith is more about giving than getting. Far too often in our Christian walk we are like children sitting on Santa's lap. We have our wish list and believe that God will give us everything on the list. The disciples had faith that Jesus would one day overthrow the Roman rule in Israel and establish His throne. This desire was not inherently evil, but it did not line up with God's plan and thus it did not produce fruit. This demonstrates how the armor of God is interlocking. You need the belt of truth in order to make effective use of the shield of faith. The truth is that we are not fighting for ourselves. We are fighting for the advancement of the Kingdom of God! For many years I quoted Hebrews 11:1 and Hebrews 11:6, but they seemed to offer no consistent value to my life. The verses sounded good and sometimes stirred my emotions, but at the end of the day, I often found nothing had changed. My life was lacking reward. Then one day this question came to mind, "If faith is the substance of things hoped for, what exactly are you hoping for?" At the time this question came to me, my answer was instant and fatally flawed. I was the pastor of a small church. My greatest desire was that my little church would grow. My desire seemed noble. In the day and time of the disciples, the overthrow of Rome seemed to be a noble cause. Noble causes are one of Satan's favorite distractions! My hope for a bigger church was a human hope and did not line up with this passage of Scripture. The reward I was seeking was inconsistent with the reward promised in Hebrews 11:6. Your faith is only as strong as the object of your faith. When you look to God as the rewarder, what reward are you longing for? Look at verse six again. Let's read it out of The New Living Translation.

Hebrew 11: 6 "So, you see, it is impossible to please God without faith. Anyone who wants to come to Him must believe that there is a God and that He rewards those who sincerely seek Him."

Pay special attention to the part that says, "Anyone who wants to come to God." What is the desire? I want to be close to God. So what is the reward? What are you hoping for above all else? The correct answer can be summed up in one word, "GOD!"

Consider Job. He had boils covering his entire body. He had lost his children. His wife had encouraged him to, "Curse God and die." His friends were comforting him by telling him how he had brought all this sickness upon himself. In the midst of all of his troubles, if you could have interviewed Job and asked the question, "Job what are you hoping for? What is it you want above all things?" You or I, if we were in his shoes, might have asked for healing or restoration with our family. We might have asked for some better friends. But, Job's greatest desire, even in the midst of intense suffering is demonstrated in his own words.

Job 19: 23 "Oh, that my words were recorded, that they were written on a scroll, 24 that they were inscribed with an iron tool on lead, or engraved in rock forever! 25 I know that my Redeemer lives, and that in the end He will stand upon the earth. 26 And after my skin has been destroyed, yet in my flesh I will see God; 27 I myself will see Him with my own eyes--I, and not another. How my heart yearns within me!"

It was Job's intense desire to draw close to God that produced his outstanding character. Character is a necessary ingredient for genuine biblical faith. To get a better understanding of this let's look at another verse in Scripture.

Romans 5: 1 "Therefore, since we have been justified through faith, we have peace with God through our Lord Jesus Christ, 2 through whom we have gained access by faith into this grace in which we now stand. And we rejoice in the hope of the glory of God. 3 Not only so, but we also rejoice in our sufferings, because we know that suffering produces perseverance; 4 perseverance, character; and character, hope. 5 And hope does not disappoint us, because God has poured out His love into our hearts by the Holy Spirit, whom He has given us."

The part of this verse I want to highlight is the relationship between hope and character. Verse four tells us that character leads to hope. You see, genuine faith is the "substance of things hoped for," and hope is a product of character. Without character you have no hope. In America most states have a lottery. People purchase these lottery tickets in spite of the unfathomable odds, looking for that one lucky break that will make them rich. These people might say they are hoping to win the jackpot. However, based on Romans 5:4-5, I propose that they truly have no hope. What they have is wishful thinking. Wishing and hoping are two different things. Wishing for something takes no character. Take some time to read and meditate on Romans 5 and Hebrews 11. Remember, genuine hope does not disappoint. The object of genuine hope is God! When your hope is to draw close to God, He will reach across any circumstance to get to you. When your hope is to draw close to Him you will never be disappointed. This hope will drive the faith that will bring you into the presence of the Almighty God. In His presence, you will discover the fullness of His love. When you find this, you have found everything! You may seek and find fame. You may seek and find healing for your body. You may seek and find restoration for a multitude of things in life, but when you find the fullness of your Father God, you have found so much more! When you seek and find God, you will find every good thing. This mindset will produce genuine biblical faith. As this thinking takes hold of your heart, you will abandon selfish ambitions. You will lock you shield with other like-minded brothers and sisters in Christ to advance the Kingdom of God! This kind of faith will be a shield that will block every fiery arrow the devil can launch at you in this day of war.

Chapter Nine

The Helmet of Salvation

Psalms 118: 14 "The LORD is my strength and song, and is become my salvation."

Before we begin dealing with the truth about salvation, let's take some time to consider the symbolism of the helmet. The purpose of the helmet is to protect the head. People wear helmets for all types of activities these days. Hard hats are worn in construction zones. Bike riders often wear helmets. In many places the law requires a motorcycle rider to wear a helmet. Helmets protect the brain from injury. This is a very simple concept in the physical, but how does it relate to the spiritual? When the demons, with whom we are warring, take shots at our head, they are going for our thoughts. The only weapon of hell is the lie. Our enemy loves to attack our thought life with his lies.

Demons do speak to us. Say that out loud in a crowd and you will get some strange looks. People struggle with the idea that the spirit realms communicate with us. It is because demons speak to us that we need the helmet of salvation. The helmet protects my thought life and keeps me free. The salvation this helmet symbolizes is more than being saved from hell or being saved to heaven. It is salvation from every evil thought that would put me in bondage. We are first and foremost spiritual beings. I love the quote, "We are not human beings having a temporary spiritual experience. We are spiritual being having a temporary human experience." In John 10:27, Jesus said, "My sheep know my voice." People have no problem with saying that "the devil tempted me." The question is how he would be able to tempt you, other than speaking to you. People say things like, "Something just told me I should take a different route to work today." I often joke that one of our nicknames for the Holy Spirit is Something. Our struggle in this area goes back to the fact that from the time of our childhood we have been taught to process things in the physical. If it is not physical, it is not real. Yet experience tells us something different. Every one has brushes with the spiritual realm that they know are real, but cannot explain. Many choose to ignore it or explain it away, but the Bible clearly teaches us that there is spiritual communication. Demons will speak to you whether you like it or not. The Holy Spirit will respect you free will. If your response to the devil is to ignore him, he is delighted and will violate you will without regard. The Holy Spirit will honor your choice. If your actions and deeds tell the Holy Spirit that you will not hear Him, then He will not speak. But when you seek Him He will speak to you. In Luke 12:12, Jesus told us that the Holy Spirit will teach you. How can He teach unless He speaks to us? Spiritual voices are seldom heard audibly. That is to say, we do not hear the demons say things in the physical realm. They are voices in our heads. That is why we need to helmet of salvation.

A few years ago, I was setting in a class room and read a poster the teacher had put up on the wall. The words on that poster read as follows:

Be careful what you think, for your thoughts become your words. Be careful what you say, for your words become your actions. Be careful what you do, for your actions become you habits. Be careful about your habits, for your habits become your character. Be careful about your character, for you character becomes your destiny.

Over the years I have shortened this down, so you can say it this way. My thoughts become my words. My words become my actions. My actions become my habits. My habits become my character and my character becomes my destiny. One verse of Scripture that backs this line of thinking can be found in Matthew 12:34 "For out of the abundance of the heart the mouth speaks." (KJV) This line of thinking puts emphasis on protecting our thought life. As we continue in this chapter you will see clearly how the helmet of salvation is vital in this regard.

When Jesus was tempted in the wilderness, it was a battle for control of Jesus' thought life. Jesus won the fight by speaking God's Word to keep

His thoughts grounded in truth. Remember, the loudest thought wins. His mind was full of the truth of God's Word. Because of being grounded in the truth, when Satan lied to Him, it immediately contradicted the truth. As soon as the contradiction occurred Jesus took action by speaking the truth and thus reinforcing it in His mind. We know Jesus won the battle that day, but there is a verse in this account that we often overlook. When Jesus had thoroughly defeated Satan, Luke tells us that Satan departed until a more opportune time. (Luke 4; 1-13) Jesus knew that He lived in the day of war. He had won the battle for that day, but Satan would come and attack His thought life many more times in the years to come. We see one of these opportune times near the end of Jesus' life.

Matthew 16: 21 "From then on Jesus began to tell His disciples plainly that He had to go to Jerusalem, and He told them what would happen to Him there. He would suffer at the hands of the leaders and the leading priests and the teachers of religious law. He would be killed, and He would be raised on the third day. 22 But Peter took Him aside and corrected Him. "Heaven forbid, Lord," he said. "This will never happen to You!" 23 Jesus turned to Peter and said, "Get away from Me, Satan! You are a dangerous trap to Me. You are seeing things merely from a human point of view, and not from God's." 24 Then Jesus said to the disciples, "If any of you wants to be My follower, you must put aside your selfish ambition, shoulder your cross, and follow Me. 25 If you try to keep your life for yourself, you will lose it. But if you give up your life for Me, you will find true life. 26 And how do you benefit if you gain the whole world but lose your own soul in the process? Is anything worth more than your soul?" (NLT)

The first thing I would like to point out from this passage is how swiftly Jesus dealt with this issue. Immediately, Jesus spoke to the situation. In line with Ephesians 6:12, which says, "We wrestle not with flesh and blood", Jesus dealt with His true enemy. His enemy was not Peter. When Jesus commanded Satan, He was not saying that Peter was Satan. He was, in fact, speaking directly to Satan. It was true that Satan was using Peter's tongue. Satan had infiltrated Peter's thought life. Only moments before this statement, Peter had made another statement. In the previous verse Peter had made the great declaration, "Thou art the Christ. The Son of the Living God." Now Peter had tuned in his spiritual dial to different frequency. Satan had placed thoughts into Peter's mind. Peter accepted those thoughts and then spoke them out loud. Jesus responded by dealing with the attack in the correct order. First He rebuked the author of the thoughts, which was Satan. Then He instructed Peter. The instruction is critical to every single battle we face. A dangerous trap is laid for us when we think merely from a human point of view. When our minds are filled with truth, God's point of view will prevail in our thinking. When the doctor tells us we are sick and that there is no cure, our response will come from God's point of view. When checkbook tells us we are not able to go on that mission trip or support a certain ministry, we will check in the spiritual realm to see what God has to say about it.

The tricky part of this mind game is identifying where thoughts originate. Not every evil thought comes from the devil. Jeremiah 17:9 tells us that the human heart is deceitful above all things. One reason Satan was successful in infiltrating Peter's thoughts was because of Peter's selfish ambitions. Peter was not interested in the spiritual kingdom that Jesus was building. He was moving in his human point of view which was that the Roman Empire needed to be overthrown. While there are many thoughts, with many different points of origin, accepting and acting on the right thoughts can be accomplished by accessing God's point of view in the matter. This takes spending time with God, searching the Scriptures with a single desire to know His will. As we fill our heads with the thoughts that come from this search, the Holy Spirit will place the helmet of salvation, which guards our thoughts, upon our heads.

Our enemy is most effective when we are unaware of his actions. If Satan had shown up in person and said to Peter, "Hey. I need your help in setting a trap for Jesus." Peter's response would have been the same as Jesus. Even with Peter's misguided motives, his love for Jesus was great and he would never cooperate willingly with any one who would try to bring harm to his Master. Satan crafted the thought that drove Peter's words, so that Peter believed he was speaking his own original thought. By the time the words came out of Peter's mouth, he had taken ownership of the thought. He was not the author of the thought, but once he accepted the thought, it became his. Once the thought was accepted, the words that followed were Peter's. They were powerful and dangerous.

One of your enemy's favorite tricks is to speak to you in the first person. If he is trying to tempt you to eat a second piece of pie, he will not say, "You should have another piece of pie." This straight on approach will often engage us and bring about an argument. Instead, he will put this thought in your head, "I should have another piece of pie." A few months later, as he attempts to erode your self-esteem, he will not say, "You are a fat pig." This statement would often invoke a defense. Instead, he will place the thought in your head, "I am a fat pig." His rate of success will be much greater with a first person approach. I used to battle some terrible ugly thoughts. I would often say to myself, "How could you think such ugly thoughts?" Countless times when I would be at a church service, some strange perverse thought would pop up in my mind. I would then battle with guilt and condemnation. How could I possibly think such ugly things, especially while in church? I finally discovered that the thoughts had not originated in my mind. My enemy fed me the thought, as though it was my own. The original thought was not what did the most damage. The thought afterwards was the one that stuck with me. How could I think such an ugly thing? The truth was that the second thought came from the same demon that had tossed the first thought at me. Once I realized this, instead of reacting in guilt and shame, I would respond to this attack by saying, out loud, "This is not my thought. I reject it. My thoughts are fixed on Jesus!" After years of being beaten down by some perverse demon spirit, I finally put on my helmet. I responded to his lie every time. It only took a few weeks and this demon left for good.

Joshua 1: 8 "This Book of the Law shall not depart from your mouth, but you shall meditate in it day and night, that you may observe to do according to all that is written in it. For then you will make your way prosperous, and then you will have good success." (KJV)

To meditate "literally" means imagine it. Draw a picture of it in you mind. As you do this with the Word of God, it will make sense to you. It is easy to obey rules when they make sense. If you tell me not to open that door over there, my immediate desire is to open the door. I want to know. This is human nature. However, if you tell me not to open that door over there because there is an angry lion on the other side, now I have no problem obeying. When you hear bits of God's Word here and there, sometimes it doesn't make much sense, but when you take time to meditate on it, you will find that its meaning will be clear. It will become a living force in your life. As you meditate on it, you will be reinforcing that helmet of salvation.

Romans 12: 2 "And do not be conformed to this world, but be transformed by the renewing of your mind, that you may prove what is that good and acceptable and perfect will of God." (KJV)

Anyone who knows me can tell you that I am an avid fan of NFL Football. I love the strategies of the game. The players in this game are the best in the world for this particular sport. Most players make several million dollars per year. Every year the teams begin to gather in late July and early August for training camp. Think about this! Most of these men are veteran players. They have been playing since they were in grade school. They are the world's best, but every season they come back to training camp. Not only that, but they practice hard every day of the week during the season. From the rookie to the most experienced veteran they practice. They are renewing their minds. Regardless of their talent, if they do not continue to renew they will get sloppy. They will be conformed. To take your stand in this day of war, you must be committed. You must renew your mind daily or the devil will come and take your helmet, by deceiving you with clever lies.

From the book of Joel, in the Old Testament to Acts, Romans and 1 Corinthians, we can read that "whoever calls on the name of the Lord will be saved." This is really good news! However, many people lack an indepth understanding of what this truly means. For many "being saved" just means I am going to Heaven when I die. It is like an insurance policy to be cashed in when the time comes. This kind of doctrine does in fact offer us something worthwhile. Going to Heaven is a good thing. In the minds of every healthy person, this is a long way off. It offers little value for today. The truth is that the salvation that comes in Jesus' name is a designed to be a daily deliverance. While my greatest hope is to spend eternity with Jesus in heaven, reality is that I need salvation in the here and now. The helmet of salvation is not given to us upon entry into heaven. We will have no use for it there. It is provided for us in the here and now. It is in this day of war that we need the helmet of salvation.

Today, across this world we live in there are countless wives and mothers who live with sexual secrets. Many suffered sexual abuse growing up. This trauma and the confusion it produces in the life of a young girl, if not dealt with, is carried into adulthood. By the time they get married and have children, they are prisoners of numerous lies. These lies bombard the thought life endlessly throughout each day. They learn to carry their chains with a certain grace. They discover ways to cope with the shame as they move through their lives. One of the problems with this kind of life is the hurt they feel. There is a saying that I have used for many years. Hurt people hurt people. Here are some of the thoughts that plague a woman in this circumstance.

- I am unlovely
- I don't deserve good things
- I can't trust anybody
- Sooner or latter they will hurt me
- I must protect myself, because no one else will
- I could have done something about it
- I must be a flawed person

This is just a short list of some of the lies that swirl in the minds of sexual abuse victims. These thoughts are the flaming arrows, lies shot from demons to keep their victims captive. To protect herself from these destructive thoughts she needs to know God's thoughts about these things.

A young man may have dealt with some of the same issues of sexual abuse. In my life it was not sexual abuse, but the abuse of bullies at school and social wars at church that left my head filled with countless lies, which affected everything from my relationship with my wife and children, down to my performance at work. I learned to defend myself with trophies and accomplishments. I created a spirit of competition in my home. I worked night and day. It was my passion to dominate in everything. From a simple game of Monopoly with my family or friends to the board room, I had a fierce sense of competition.

To this day I am vulnerable to the insecurities that come with that kind of life, so I put on my helmet of salvation. I fill my head with the truth about grace and mercy and unconditional love. I proclaim aloud the truth, that God loved me with all of His love before I ever did anything. I renew my mind with Romans 5:8, which tells me that while I was at my worst, Christ died for me. God will not love me more or less, based on my performance! This is salvation! This truth guards my thought life. So when Jesus died on the cross, He saved my soul from hell. His blood made a way for me to go to heaven! But, Jesus also saved me from the hatred I felt as a little boy with a busted lip and a bloody nose. He saved me from the life time of pain from being rejected by father figures in church. He saved the rape victim from the life of anger, fear and un-forgiveness. The great salvation mentioned in Hebrews 2:3 is not for the sweet by and by. It is for the here and now!

Luke 4:17 "He found the place where it was written: 18 'The Spirit of the Lord is upon Me, Because He has anointed Me To preach the gospel to the poor; He has sent Me to heal the brokenhearted, To proclaim liberty to the captives And recovery of sight to the blind, To set at liberty those who are oppressed; 19 To proclaim the acceptable year of the Lord.' 20 Then He closed the book, and gave it back to the attendant and sat down. And the eyes of all who were in the synagogue were fixed on Him. 21 And He began to say to them, 'Today this Scripture is fulfilled in your hearing.' "

Jesus did not conclude this reading by saying, "When you die and go to heaven these things will happen." He proclaimed, "Today this Scripture is fulfilled in your hearing."

I have been saved from every mistake that my parents might have made! I have been saved from all the intentions of the bullies in school. I have been saved from my own stupid choices, past, present and future! This truly is a great salvation. So as I listen to a fellow minister's introduction of me right before I preach and the devil begins to say to me, "If only he knew. If he knew about the time you did this or the time you thought that. You're no good for this job. How could you after..." I adjust my helmet slightly as I say out loud, "Isaiah 54:17 says my righteousness is of God." I remind myself that 2 Corinthians 12:9 says, "His strength is made perfect in our weakness." I will reinforce the truth in my life that according to Philippians 4:13, "I can do all things through Christ who strengthens me." And maybe for a dash of humility I will recite John 15:5, "Without Him I can do no good thing." These same thoughts save me from condemnation when I look at mistakes I have made raising my children.

When I emphasize that the Word is most powerful when spoken, you need to understand that volume is not vital in the spiritual realm. It is not how loud you say it. It's not even how emotional you are when you speak.

What gives your words power in the spirit realm is truth and faith. I can whisper those words ever so softly as I proceed to the platform. I have spoken the Word while with clients in the business world. I have recited Scripture and even prayed in tongues as I walked the halls of the placement facility where I worked for three years. There are also times when I cry out with passion, but I am not limited to those times when it comes to the power of the spoken Word.

From the age of Roman soldiers to NFL football players of today, helmets are used to intimidate the enemy. When, by the power of the Holy Spirit, you take the Helmet of Salvation and place it on your head, you become an intimidating warrior to your enemy. With your thought life carefully protected by the truth of God's Word you will walk in the salvation He provided by the completed work of Calvary. Your enemy will grow weary of throwing lies at your head as one by one you repel each of them with the truth. Your confidence will grow and his will dwindle as you stand your ground in this day of war.

Chapter Ten

The Sword of the Spirit

Ephesians 6:17 "Take the sword of the Spirit, which is the Word of God."

When I was a young boy I watched an event with my family that I will never forget. It took place outside our dining room window. Our family watched as a pair of mocking birds was teaching one of their babies how to fly. During this process a cat showed up. The cat immediately zeroed in on the baby mocking bird. As the cat approach his target the mommy and daddy mocking bird protected their baby. It was incredible to watch what these birds could do. They came at that cat from every angle. At times it seemed that there was a complete army of birds attacking this cat. After a few minutes the cat gave up. Then the baby mocking bird did something very foolish. Having watched the actions of his mom and dad, he decided to dive bomb the cat. As he did this he bounced of the cat and fell to the ground dangerously close to this predator. The cat was so badly beaten down by the attack of the adult birds that he just laid there. The little bird repeated his foolish actions several times. The whole time the old cat just laid there. He knew that Mom and Dad were watching and that if he made any move towards this baby bird he would lose more fur. The baby bird had a misguided confidence which led him to the false assumption that he had the power to mess with this cat the way he had seen his parents do. The truth is, had it not been for protection of mom and dad, this confident little bird would have been eaten. This story paints a vivid picture of many immature spiritual warriors. More than once in my own life, I have been like that little baby mocking bird. I thought I was doing battle with the enemy, when in fact; my actions were foolishness which required my Father in heaven to protect me from being devoured. For a young baby immaturity is to be expected. However, swords are not for babies.

Throughout history the sword has been a symbol of military might. The sword is symbolic of power and authority. Kings had unique swords. When the king's sword was raised his officers would recognize it. At the center of the legend of Camelot, there was a sword. This sword was the sword of King Arthur. It stood for the values and interests of King Arthur. As we unfold this teaching on the Sword, we are going to build on the two points found in Ephesians 6:17. These two points are The Sword is of the Spirit and The Sword is the Word of God.

What does it mean to be of the Spirit? If some one says, "That was of God?" what exactly are we saying? To clearly understand what it means to be of the Spirit, let's look at the definition of the word "of". According to Dictionary.com the word "of" is used to indicate cause, motive, occasion, or reason. For example, to die of hunger. Without an intimate relationship with the Holy Spirit you cannot not know His motives or reasons. Galatians 5:17 – 26 gives some insight on what the Holy Spirit's motive or reason is.

Galatians 5: 22 "But when the Holy Spirit controls our lives, He will produce this kind of fruit in us: love, joy, peace, patience, kindness, goodness, faithfulness, 23 gentleness, and self-control. Here there is no conflict with the law. 24 Those who belong to Christ Jesus have nailed the passions and desires of their sinful nature to His cross and crucified them there. 25 If we are living now by the Holy Spirit, let us follow the Holy Spirit's leading in every part of our lives." (NLT)

When most of us think of a sword, we do not envision love, joy, peace, kindness, goodness, faithfulness, gentleness or self-control. These are always the motives of the Holy Spirit.

The physical swords we can see with our eyes are made to wound and kill. A spiritual sword can wound the righteous, but it does not kill. You cannot kill a demon. We know from God's Word that they will live forever in the lake of fire. The Sword of the Spirit will not kill and it will only wound the hearts of men and women who are sensitive to God's Word.

I hope at this point I have you thinking a little. So what do I do with a sword that will not kill and only wounds people with a good conscious? I will explain a little later in this chapter. For now let us stay focused on the topic "of the Spirit."

Staying in the Spirit in the heat of battle is not easy. You must begin and end every spiritual battle IN THE SPIRIT! Many battles begin in the Spirit, but as the battle rages offense enters and soon we are fighting for selfish reasons. The Holy Spirit does not falter in His motives or reason. His motive is the same today as it was when Jesus walked the earth. He is never swayed by emotion. While there is often violence and even anger in the battle, His motive is to bring forth the spiritual fruit talked about in Galatians 5. Jesus demonstrated all kinds of emotions in His ministry. While He experienced these emotions, His actions were never motivated by emotion. His actions were totally controlled by the Holy Spirit. His anger was apparent as He drove the money changers out of the temple, but His actions were not driven by anger. Rather, His anger stemmed from the fact that the fruit of the Spirit was being impeded. His motive, as He turned over the tables and drove out the merchants, was to restore the fruit of the Spirit. Pay special attention to the repetition of the phrase, "of the Spirit." The moment you are not moving of and by the Spirit you forfeit the Sword of The Spirit.

The Sword is the Word of God.

The Sword of the Spirit is symbolic of God's Word. Literally the Sword of the Spirit is the Word of God. Therefore, we are equipped with the Sword of the Spirit when, by the power of the Holy Spirit, we speak God's Word concerning an event or action.

John 14: 26 "But when the Father sends the Counselor as My representative -- and by the Counselor, I mean the Holy Spirit -- He will teach you everything and will remind you of everything I Myself have told you."

In order for the Holy Spirit to remind us of the words of Jesus, we must first store those words up in our hearts. You cannot be reminded of something of which you have never been made aware. There will be times that you find yourself under attack. This is not the time to sit down and study God's Word. It is time to know and act, by the power of the Holy

Spirit. If your knowledge of God's Word is limited, the best He can do is protect you from the enemy. You will be like the little mocking bird I wrote about at the beginning of this chapter. When you are deep in the Word of God, it will be deep in you. Store up the Word of God in your heart. When you have a rich abundance of God's Word in you heart, then when the battle breaks out, the Holy Spirit will begin to call up the right words at the right time. This is the Sword of the Spirit.

It is not enough to know the Bible. You may have a rich knowledge of it, but you must let the Holy Spirit direct you. The Pharisees knew the Scripture almost as well as Jesus, but in spite of this, they were ignorant and foolish. The Apostle Paul knew the Scriptures well. This did not stop him from writing in 1st Corinthians 13:12, that "we peer through a glass dimly." He was acknowledging that even with all his knowledge and wisdom, he was still very much in the dark without the help of the Holy Spirit.

There was a woman at the first church that I pastored who had been healed of cancer. She had a wonderful testimony. After doctors had given her a limited time to live the Holy Spirit reminded her of a verse in Scripture. Psalms 118:17 "I will not die, but I will live to tell what the LORD has done." (NLT) She began to repeat this verse over and over until she felt that God had healed her. This was a well-documented miracle. She had lived cancer-free for several years by the time I heard this wonderful testimony. She had taken the mighty Sword of the Spirit and driven cancer out of her life! I do not know where this woman is now or how her health is. I do know that some day that death will come for her and she can recite Psalms 118:17 with all her might, but it will not change things. It is appointed to all of us to die. The point I want to make with this story is that the Scriptures come to life when we are directed by the Holy Spirit. The Bible is not a book of incantations that can be used at the will of human beings to direct the events of life. We must read the Bible. We must study and search for the deep things of God. We need to store it up richly in our hearts, but we must know that the Holy Spirit is the One Who will remind us. This is to say that the Holy Spirit is still calling the shots. The Holy Spirit will take the deposit of God's Word in your heart and give you the power to prevail in every battle according to His good plan. The word of God will enable you to move according to His plan. It will not subjugate God to your plan.

Luke 6:45 "A good man out of the good treasure of his heart bringeth forth that which is good; and an evil man out of the evil treasure of his heart bringeth forth that which is evil: for of the abundance of the heart his mouth speaketh."

Consider these following three scriptures as we move on.

Joshua 1: 8 "Yes, keep this book of the Torah on your lips, and meditate on it day and night, so that you will take care to act according to everything written in it. Then your undertakings will prosper, and you will succeed." (Complete Jewish Bible)

2nd Corinthians 10: 3 "For though we walk in the flesh, we do not war according to the flesh. 4 For the weapons of our warfare are not carnal but mighty in God for pulling down strongholds, 5 casting down arguments and every high thing that exalts itself against the knowledge of God, bringing every thought into captivity to the obedience of Christ, 6 and being ready to punish all disobedience when your obedience is fulfilled." (KJV)

The preceding Scriptures tell us to store up God's Word in our hearts. When we spend time in God's Word, we are under its influence. When events of this world tell us one thing and God's Word says another, the Sword of the Spirit comes out of our mouths.

The Sword of the Spirit Pierces and Divides

Hebrews 7: 12 "For the Word of God is living and active. Sharper than any double-edged sword, it penetrates even to dividing soul and spirit, joints and marrow; it judges the thoughts and attitudes of the heart." (NIV)

The sword of the Spirit does not work like a physical sword. In the beginning of this chapter I mentioned that The Sword of the Spirit will only wound people with a conscience. I have been wounded by the Sword of the Spirit many times in my life. There are many times the Sword of the Spirit has come and pierced my heart. There is a biblical example of the Sword of the Spirit piercing a person with a conscience in 2nd Samuel 12: 1-15. David has sinned with Bathsheba and murdered her husband. Only God knew all the gruesome details. David was keeping secrets, so God spoke to His prophet Nathan. Nathan then confronted David.

2nd Samuel 12:1-14 1 "Then the Lord sent Nathan to David. And he came to him, and said to him: 'There were two men in one city, one rich and the other poor. 2 The rich man had exceedingly many flocks and herds. 3 But the poor man had nothing, except one little ewe lamb which he had bought and nourished; and it grew up together with him and with his children. It ate of his own food and drank from his own cup and lay in his bosom; and it was like a daughter to him. 4 And a traveler came to the rich man, who refused to take from his own flock and from his own herd to prepare one for the wayfaring man who had come to him; but he took the poor man's lamb and prepared it for the man who had come to him.' 5 So David's anger was greatly aroused against the man, and he said to Nathan, 'As the Lord lives, the man who has done this shall surely die! 6 And he shall restore fourfold for the lamb, because he did this thing and because he had no pity.' 7 Then Nathan said to David, 'You are the man!' Thus says the Lord God of Israel: 'I anointed you king over Israel, and I delivered you from the hand of Saul. 8 I gave you your master's house and your master's wives into your keeping, and gave you the house of Israel and Judah. And if that had been too little, I also would have given you much more! 9 Why have you despised the commandment of the Lord, to do evil in His sight? You have killed Uriah the Hittite with the sword; you have taken his wife to be your wife, and have killed him with the sword of the people of Ammon. 10 Now therefore, the sword shall never depart from your house, because you have despised Me, and have taken the wife of Uriah the Hittite to be your wife.' 11 Thus says the Lord: 'Behold, I will raise up adversity against you from your own house; and I will take your wives before your eyes and give them to your neighbor, and he shall lie with your wives in the sight of this sun. 12 For you did it secretly, but I will do this thing before all Israel, before the sun.' 13 So David said to Nathan, 'I have sinned against the Lord.' And Nathan said to David, 'The Lord also has put away your sin; you shall not die.' " (KJV)

The words God gave Nathan pierced David's heart. David responded by repenting. David was keeping everything secret and living with the weight of the shame until God's Word came and pierced his heart and brought repentance. When David repented the sword of the Spirit which is God's Word separated him from his sin. This is a very delicate procedure. You will not be able to pierce and divide without the guidance of the Holy Spirit. Only by the power and grace of the Holy Spirit can we demonstrate Proverbs 27:6, which says, "faithful are the wounds of a friend."

Jesus pierced Peter's heart. When Peter was filled with pride and making claims he could not keep, Jesus spoke words that humbled him. When Jesus prophesied that Peter would deny knowing Jesus before the cock crowed twice, He wounded Peter. After Peter fulfilled the prophecy, he was broken by these same words. The brokenness paved the way for Peter's restoration. Psalms 51:17 tells us that a broken and contrite heart is the sacrifice God is looking for.

Now let's put this into the context of spiritual warfare. Jesus came to destroy the works of the devil. Both King David and Peter were pierced by the Word of God. Both men were wounded and broken, which led to restoration and freedom from the work of the devil in their lives. This is not the sensational Hollywood exorcism many think of when it comes to spiritual warfare. It is genuine and life changing. I am not discounting exorcisms where demons manifest. I have seen these things happen. What I am saying is that it is often less sensational than we might expect. If you are just hunting for demons, you have a very limited concept of what true spiritual warfare is. When you have mastered the less sensational aspect of spiritual warfare, you will be more than able to handle times when the supernatural manifests in dramatic ways. There are many accounts in the Bible where demons acted. They cried out when Jesus came near. They taunted the Apostle Paul in Acts 16. These same demons are still active today and must be confronted, but we are not demon hunters. We are hunting for lost souls. When demons get in our way we deal with them, but we must never let them distract us.

When we have stored up the Word of God in our heart and then submitted ourselves fully to the Holy Spirit, He will put God's Word in our mouth. When this happens, we will separate sickness from people. We will separate demons from their place of authority.

Luke 11: 21 "When a strong man, fully armed, guards his own palace, his goods are in peace. 22 But when a stronger than he comes upon him and overcomes him, he takes from him all his armor in which he trusted, and divides his spoils." (NIV)

When we are fully suited in the armor with the Sword of the Spirit in our mouths, we are the "stronger than he." We will use the Sword of the Spirit to separate the devil from his strongholds. We will separate the demons from their goods. By the grace of God, we will set the captive free! Always remember, this is what the fight is all about. When we use the Sword of the Spirit to pierce, we will have a cautious and humble spirit. When we use the Sword of the Spirit to separate, it will never be for selfish gain. Our heart's desire will be to separate souls from the kingdom of darkness and to bring them into the marvelous light. This is what the fight is all about in this Day of War.

Chapter Eleven

Prayer

Luke 18: 1 "… men always ought to pray
and not lose heart" (NKJ)

One of the most defining aspects of the life of Jesus was His prayer life. We know from the Gospels that is was a normal practice for Jesus to pray throughout the night. One of the most notable actions of Jesus was when He cleansed the temple.

Matthew 21: 12 "Then Jesus went into the temple of God and drove out all those who bought and sold in the temple, and overturned the tables of the money changers and the seats of those who sold doves. 13 And He said to them, 'It is written, My house shall be called a house of prayer, but you have made it a den of thieves.' " (KJV)

When Jesus said, "it is written," He was referring to the writings of Isaiah.

Isaiah 56: 7 "Even them I will bring to My holy mountain, And make them joyful in My house of prayer. Their burnt offerings and their sacrifices will be accepted on My altar; For My house shall be called a house of prayer for all nations." (KJV)

We see here that Jesus and God have the same view in regards to prayer. If you do some study of the temple, you will learn that the merchants had set up their marketing in the part of the temple called the "Court of the Gentiles." This was a part of the temple where both Jews and Gentiles were allowed. Gentiles were not allowed in other parts of the temple. The merchants, who were buying and selling, had demonstrated a complete lack of respect for those Gentiles who wished to offer up prayers in the temple. You see, the Jews were God's chosen people. They knew this. While they believed this, and rightly so, most of them never came to the understanding of why they were chosen. To be chosen can be a big honor, especially if the One Who has chosen you is the Almighty God! But, what were they chosen for? The actions in the temple demonstrated their ignorance of this truth. They were chosen by God to become the nation through which the Messiah, the Savior of the world, would be born. Many of the religious of that day despised the Gentiles. Their disdain and disrespect was demonstrated clearly by the fact that the action of the merchants, in the Court of the Gentiles was accepted.

There is an attitude and a behavior that are revealed in this event that are evident in the modern church. The attitude was one of privilege and not service. In Jesus' day Jews had little regard for those who were outside their faith. God had chosen to bless them as a nation and make them powerful, so they could bring the Light of Heaven to the whole world. But they had become self-absorbed. Instead of looking on the gentiles as lost souls in need of a savior, they looked down on them as second-class human-beings and judged them. God's heart was that His temple would be a house of prayer for all nations, but the Jewish people had different priorities.

I worked for three years at a detention center for "at risk" teen girls. It was some of the most rewarding work I have ever done. I saw lives that had been ravaged and abused in ways I could never have imagined. These young women would arrive at our facility so angry, so hurt, and so lost. The program was a 12 month, 4 stage plan. A majority of the girls who came into the program would complete the fourth stage and be successfully discharged. It was a secular program, and whereas we were not permitted to evangelize, it was permitted to talk to the students if they asked questions. They had a constitutional right to pursue their faith. During the three years I worked there, I was privileged to lead many of these young ladies to Jesus. Discharge was a critical time for these young people. Many of them would go back to the same home and the same community where they had gotten into trouble. At one point in my tenure, I put together a plan to help these girls find a good church. I would sit down with the young lady and look up five churches in her area. We would pick churches that she felt would be the best for her. I would then have her write a letter to the youth pastors. In the letter I prompted them to touch lightly on their troubled past and the progress they had made in turning their life around. I then added my own letter requesting help in setting up a pen pal. My idea was to help facilitate a positive friendship for my student that could develop and grow before she arrived back home. It would have to be someone who would meet her with excitement upon her arrival and help her enter into church fellowship. The results were devastating. Even now I tear up as I recall the impact. I used this plan with five different young ladies. Five brand new baby Christians looking for help. Each of the five ladies mailed out five letters to five different churches. These were girls from three different states. Out of the twenty-five letters that were mailed, we received zero responses. Most of these churches had lovely websites. They had pictures and events. They had youth pastors and children's pastors. They had youth buildings, but they did not have the time or the passion to respond to a young teenager who needed their help. I know there are churches out there that would respond differently. My point is not to say all churches are bad. I do believe that our modern church struggles with priorities. I believe that several youth pastors were excited when they first received the letter, but set it to the side and forgot about it. I believe their intentions were good, but they had too many things going on. They had their own kids to worry about. This is the same attitude from the temple in Jesus' day. We have our own to worry about. I propose to you that the remedy for this attitude is prayer. Remember God said in Isaiah, "My House shall be called a House of prayer." This may sound overly simple, but I believe it needs to be pointed out. The reason a house would be called a house of prayer was because people called it a house of prayer. People would only do this for one of two reasons. One, there is a sign on it that says, house of prayer. I don't believe this is what God had in mind. Second, because the people of that house have a reputation for prayer that gets results. James 5:16 tells us, "The effective prayer of a righteous man avails much." (NKJ)

I have the privilege of knowing about a special prayer chain in the Tampa, Florida area. I am privileged because I have been put on that prayer chain a number of times, and every time the results have been significant. These ladies have been praying together for over 20 years. People from all over the world call to have these ladies pray. This is how our churches should be. I only know one of the ladies from this group. She and her husband have been special friends to my family for many years. I do not know any of the others. All I know about them is they pray effectively. The reason I know about them is, unlike the religious Jews of Jesus day, they have reached out to people outside their own little group. I pointed out in the beginning of this book that our armor is not for defense. We are not called to fight a selfish little war for our own comfort and safety. This day of war is not about me and mine getting everything we want and living a life of privilege. If we are to be Christ-like warriors, our concern will be for those people outside our cozy church walls that are being tormented and destroyed by our enemy, the devil. Our fight will be to advance the Kingdom of our Friend and Savior, Jesus Christ! The attitude far too often is, I have my own things to worry about. This leads to a selfish behavior, which turns prayer into a boring session of asking God to do stuff.

Today churches are known for their fantastic buildings, or their charismatic preacher. Perhaps they have the best praise and worship team or a large dynamic youth group. Where is the church that people pause for a moment and then say, "Oh, now there is a house of prayer!" The first church I pastured had a banner up in the fellowship hall. It simply said, "Prayer Changes Things." So I had a prayer meeting. Less than ten percent of the people showed up. This kind of behavior has been part of every church of which I have ever been a part. Have a special speaker, a concert or some sort of special seasonal program and you can pack the house, but call a special prayer meeting and all you'll need is a small Sunday School room. One church I attended would have between two and three thousand people in attendance every Sunday morning. I attended many of the prayer meetings when I was a part of this church. Attendance was usually around twenty people.

Why is this? I believe it is because people have been repeatedly disappointed when they have prayed. I will also tell you that most people find prayer to be boring. Fervent effective prayer comes from the heart of a servant. The only effective spiritual warrior is a person with a strong prayer life. The only person with a strong prayer life is one who has the heart of a servant.

The foundational Scripture for this book has been Ephesians chapter six. Paul concludes the symbolism of the armor with this instruction:

Ephesians 6: 18 "Pray at all times and on every occasion in the power of the Holy Spirit. Stay alert and be persistent in your prayers for all Christians everywhere. 19 And pray for me, too. Ask God to give me the right words as I boldly explain God's secret plan that the Good News is for the Gentiles, too."

I have been through many teachings on prayer. Most have not been helpful and some have crippled my prayer life for a season. I could fill many pages with the wrong things I have been taught over the years, but let's skip that and get to the good stuff.

I will touch on few things that I have been taught about prayer which were not fruitful. There is a common doctrine of prayer that deals with the time of day, the length of prayer and the place. I have been taught that you should set aside a portion of time in the morning. This is the first part of your day and you should always honor God with your first fruits. This was always a problem for me. I am not a morning person. It might well be the first part of the day, but the Bible also teaches us to give the best part. If you wanted to spend some quality time with me, I can assure you early morning isn't the best. I notice in the Bible that Jesus prayed late into the night. Ephesians 6:18 tells us to pray at all times. 1 Thessalonians 5:17, tells us to pray without ceasing. How in the world can I do that? I have been taught to pray for one hour. I have also been charged to tithe my time in prayer, which would mean I would need to pray 2.4 hours every day. I have been told that I need a prayer closet. All of these teachings did more harm to my prayer life than good. All of these teaching made prayer a tedious chore. All of these teachings produced bondage in my life.

Most of the teaching I have been exposed to, concerning prayer, has been shallow and off base. An example of this is the teaching about a prayer closet. You may not have been in this school, but the lesson goes something like this. Prepare a special place where you go every day, a prayer closet. They base their misguided teaching on this passage of scripture.

Matthew 6: 6 "But thou, when thou prayest, enter into thy closet, and when thou hast shut thy door, pray to thy Father which is in secret; and thy Father which seeth in secret shall reward thee openly." (KJV)

Some translations say room instead of closet. Others imply to withdraw to a secret place, by yourself. The Jews of that day heard something totally different. First of all we must understand that the instruction Jesus was giving had nothing to do with location. He was challenging a common practice of the religious leaders who made an open show of their prayers. For the sake of time I am going to be very brief in my explanation of this passage. My hope in touching on this is that I will stir up your desire to know more. If this happens you can gain a great deal of knowledge with Google and YouTube.

When we read the word closet in the King James Version of this verse, we should understand that houses in that location and time period did not have closets as we know them. The Jewish person would have heard Jesus say, when you pray go into your tameion, which is Greek for secret chamber. The Jewish person would have understood that Jesus was talking about, what we would call the prayer shawl. In the Jewish world they are called a Tallit. This is a Hebrew word. Tall means tent. It means little. Literally it means little tent. When a Jewish man would pray he would raise his tallit above his head and close it in around his face. This symbolized being completely surrounded by the presence of the Lord. It also symbolized shutting out the world. When the man would touch corners together shutting outside world out, this is known as shutting the door. This is also referred to as a prayer closet. It was part of the Law of Moses that these people should go to the temple to pray. Jesus was not telling them to go home and get in there closets. He was telling them to block out the rest of the world. He was telling them not to concern themselves with what other people thought. He was telling them to wrap their face in their tallit and to get lost in the presence of God! Wow! What a change in the message! That does not sound boring or legalistic.

So what is prayer?

Our English word for prayer has been compromised. What I mean by that is it has lost its ability to put the right picture in our minds. Let me use another word to give you an example of what I am trying to say. In 1950 the word gay generated a certain picture in people's mind when it was used. Today that same word generates a much different picture. With this in mind let me run you through a quick little word game.

I love to watch football.

I love pizza.

I love the smell in the air on a crisp fall morning.

I love my wife.

Reading this might give you the idea that I feel the same about my wife as I do about football. The word love has lost a great deal of its meaning over the centuries.

Buddhist pray.

Hindu people pray.

Christians pray.

Even unbelievers pray.

But some Christians really pray.

With this in mind let's repair this word prayer, so that it conveys the right picture in our mind. Read each of the Scriptures listed below. See if you can pick out the common word in each of the passages.

- Genesis 3:8 "And they heard the voice of the LORD God walking in the garden in the cool of the day" (KJV)
- Genesis 5:24 "And Enoch walked with God: and he was not; for God took him." (KJV)
- Genesis 6:9 "Noah was a just man and perfect in his generations, and Noah walked with God." (KJV)
- Genesis 17:1 "And when Abram was ninety years old and nine, the LORD appeared to Abram, and said unto him, 'I am the Almighty God; walk before Me, and be thou perfect.'" (KJV)
- Genesis 48: 15 "And he blessed Joseph, and said , God, before Whom my fathers Abraham and Isaac did walk , the God which fed me all my life long unto this day," (KJV)
- Leviticus 26:12 "And I will walk among you, and will be your God, and ye shall be My people." (KJV)
- 1 Kings 8: 25 "Therefore now, LORD God of Israel, keep with Thy servant David my father that Thou promised him, saying , 'There shall not fail thee a man in My sight to sit on the throne of Israel; so that thy children take heed to their way, that they walk before Me as thou hast walked before Me.'" (KJV)

There are several more like these, but I have given you a healthy list. Did you notice the word, walk? Imagine you are at the home of a good friend for dinner and an evening of fellowship. Now imagine after dinner your friend stands and says to you, "Come, walk with me." Frequently at my house my wife will ask me if I would like to go for a walk with her. There is an old expression that includes the words, walk of life. For example; Many foreign missionaries have chosen a difficult walk of life.

In the Hebrew language, the root word for walk is halak. This word definition of this word has a list of obvious meanings, but there are a few words in the long list that stand out, such as behave, all along, on continual and to be conversant. My studies of the definition, combined with the Scriptures listed above have brought me to this explanation. Genuine biblical prayer is being continually conversant with God. It is a close intimate conversation that never comes to a conclusion.

In my life I have had some deep meaningful conversations with friends and family. Many times I have been with a friend where we would talk for hours. Finally, we would get up and walk towards the door in an attempt to wrap up the conversation. There have been times that the sun has come up and we were still talking, but in every single case the conversation did come to a conclusion. Physical limits limit our conversation and fellowship with friends and family. But in my spiritual walk with God, there is never any reason for the conversation to conclude. So when the Apostle Paul tells up to pray without ceasing, he means it in a literal way. By the shed blood of Jesus, the veil has been torn! I don't need a prayer shawl or a special room. These symbols are beautiful and if people desire to use them to portray a clearer picture of their relationship with God, that can be a wonderful thing. However, with or without these symbols, God wants me to walk with Him. I only go for walks with people who are special to me. From the garden of Eden to this very time, God's desire is to go for a walk with us.

When I hear some one boast of how many hours they prayed last week, I feel sorry for them. They are missing the big picture. For them prayer is a ritual or ceremony. If you are married and still passionately in love with you mate, imagine setting up a schedule with them. Imagine looking into the eye of your spouse on your wedding night and saying, "Now that we are married, I am going to spend 2.4 hours with you every day." Imagine her response. "We will meet in the closet, with a timer." Okay, maybe I am going a bit overboard. I hope you get the picture.

When prayer becomes a walk of life for you everything changes. For those people who pray as a ritual or ceremony two-hour prayer meetings seems like weeks. When you get a few people together who are in the middle of a never ending conversation with their Creator, a prayer meeting can go all night long. I can honestly say that in my life, prayer is the best of the best. I never eat alone. Even when I travel without Lisa, my Abba Father is there with me. I talk to Him about the meal. I tell Him about my day. I tell Him often how beautiful the sunset is and how awesome He must be to design such and awesome show. I love to watch a lightning storm with Him. This is all prayer! I do bring my requests to Him, but the time I spend making requests is minimal when compared to all the other things we talk about. Petitions and request would be boring and dry if not for the fact that I know Him intimately and this gives me confidence that He hears me when I cry and He cares!

Live it and I will loose you.

In Luke Chapter 11, Jesus was praying. When He finished, the Bible says one of His disciples asked Him to teach them how to pray. Jesus gave them, what we know as the Lord's Prayer. A better title would be The Model Prayer. You can find the Lord's Prayer in John Chapter 17. This was the second time Jesus had publicly recited this prayer. The first time He instructed us to pray this way is in the Gospel of Matthew.

Matthew 6: 5 "And when you pray, do not be like the hypocrites, for they love to pray standing in the synagogues and on the street corners to be seen by men. I tell you the truth; they have received their reward in full. 6 But when you pray, go into your room, close the door and pray to your Father, who is unseen. Then your Father, Who sees what is done in secret, will reward you. 7 And when you pray, do not keep on babbling like pagans, for they think they will be heard because of their many words. 8 Do not be like them, for your Father knows what you need before you ask Him. 9 This, then, is how you should pray: 'Our Father in heaven, hallowed be Your name, 10 Your kingdom come, Your will be done on earth as it is in heaven. 11 Give us today our daily bread. 12 Forgive us our debts, as we also have forgiven our debtors. 13 And lead us not into temptation, but deliver us from the evil one.'" (KJV)

Like many Christians, I learned this prayer when I was very young. I remember kneeling and praying this prayer with my football team during my high school days. Throughout the first thirty years of my life I recited this prayer thousands of time. Not one time did I ever feel or see any significant results. Then one morning I woke up to that still small voice that speaks to my spirit. The instruction was simple. "Live it and I will loose you." This got my attention. It was around 5:00 in the morning, which was much earlier than I normally got up. I got out of bed and went to my living room to pray and see what God meant with this instruction. The question was live what? I waited for God on this for several weeks. I searched past sermons. I scanned books. I listened extra closely to the sermons at my church or on the radio. During this time the urgency of the instruction did not fade, it grew. My thoughts were dominated throughout the day with the burning question; Live what? One reason this instruction took such a hold on my life, was because for a very long time, God had put a hold on my ministry. Each time I would attempt to resist this God would gently tell me that He was the One restraining me. I believed when I heard this instruction, God was ready to turn me loose! Finally one night I was working on a sermon outline for the Friday night prison service I taught weekly. I was reading over The Model Prayer, when the Holy Spirit said to me, "Live it and I will loose you." Suddenly this tired old poem came to life! My heart raised and my hands shook as I carefully outlined the lifestyle of this Model Prayer. My prayer life has never been the same!

In these next few pages I will outline the eleven components of the Lord's Prayer and then briefly explain how to make each component a part of the way you live.

The Eleven Components of the Lord's Prayer

1. Our
2. Father
3. Which Art in Heaven
4. Hallowed be Thy Name
5. Thy Kingdom come
6. Thy will be done on earth as it is in heaven
7. Give us this day our daily bread
8. Forgive us our debts as we forgive our debtors
9. Lead us not into temptation but, deliver us from evil
10. For Thine is the Kingdom and the power and the glory forever
11. Amen

As we look at these eleven components of pray, it is important to understand that each component is a vital part of the whole. You cannot excel in four or five and forget the rest. Think of this as a recipe for prayer. If you leave out one or two of the ingredients you will not have a favorable end result. Much like the suit of armor, the most important part is the one you neglect.

1. Our – Denotes Unity

This first word sets the tone for this entire prayer. *Our*, denotes unity. As you continue on in the prayer you will see that we pray for, "Our daily bread." We ask that we (plural) be forgiven and we ask our Father to lead us not into temptation. One of the most common themes in the Bible is unity. God desire that His children get along.

Psalms 133: 1 A song for the ascent to Jerusalem. A psalm of David. "How wonderful it is, how pleasant, when brothers live together in harmony! 2 For harmony is as precious as the fragrant anointing oil that was poured over Aaron's head, that ran down his beard and onto the border of his robe. 3 Harmony is as refreshing as the dew from Mount Hermon that falls on the mountains of Zion. And the LORD has pronounced His blessing, even life forevermore."

When we do not get along with our brothers and sisters in Christ God still loves us, but our relationship is strained. I am His child. I was bought with the shed blood of Jesus. The same blood that was shed for my sin was also shed for the sin of that brother or sister in Christ with whom I have unresolved issues. If you have children imagine someone wanting to be your good friend. While they really like you and enjoy spending time with you, they have negative feelings concerning your children. They ask that when you come to see them that you leave your kids with someone else, or if they are going to come to your house they want to make sure it is at a time when your children will not be around. It is possible to have empathy towards someone like this, but it is impossible to have a healthy relationship with them.

It is difficult to condense the teaching on this topic to the time and space we have. I encourage you to take some time apart from this book and study unity. Do a word search in your Bible study time and see what the Bible has to say about unity. No passage of Scripture gives us any clearer look into Jesus' heart on this matter than John Chapter 17. This is the prayer Jesus prayed with His disciples moments before He was betrayed and arrested. Jesus knew as He began this prayer He only had a few more moments with His friends before His death. Knowing this gives more weight to the words of this beautiful prayer. Look for the heart Jesus had for unity as you read.

John 17
Jesus Prays for Himself

1 "After Jesus said this, He looked toward heaven and prayed: 'Father, the time has come. Glorify Your Son, that Your Son may glorify You. 2 For You granted Him authority over all people that He might give eternal life to all those You have given Him. 3 Now this is eternal life: that they may know You, the only true God, and Jesus Christ, Whom You have sent. 4 I have brought you glory on earth by completing the work You gave Me to do.' "

Jesus Prays for His Disciples

5 "And now, Father, glorify Me in Your presence with the glory I had with You before the world began. 6 I have revealed You to those whom You gave Me out of the world. They were Yours; You gave them to Me and they have obeyed Your Word. 7 Now they know that everything You have given Me comes from You. 8 For I gave them the words You gave Me and they accepted them. They knew with certainty that I came from You, and they believed that You sent Me. 9 I pray for them. I am not praying for the world, but for those You have given Me, for they are Yours. 10 All I have is Yours, and all You have is Mine. And glory has come to Me through them. 11 I will remain in the world no longer, but they are still in the world, and I am coming to You. Holy Father, protect them by the power of Your name--the name You gave Me--**so that they may be one as We are one**. 12 While I was with them, I protected them and kept them safe by that name You gave Me. None has been lost except the one doomed to destruction so that Scripture would be fulfilled. 13 I am coming to You now, but I say these things while I am still in the world, so that they may have the full measure of My joy within them. 14 I have given them Your Word and the

world has hated them, for they are not of the world any more than I am of the world. 15 My prayer is not that You take them out of the world but that You protect them from the evil one. 16 They are not of the world, even as I am not of it. 17 Sanctify them by the truth; Your Word is truth. 18 As you sent Me into the world, I have sent them into the world."

Jesus Prays for All Believers

19 "For them I sanctify Myself, that they too may be truly sanctified. 20 My prayer is not for them alone. I pray also for those who will believe in Me through their message, 21 that all of them may be one, Father, just as You are in Me and I am in You. May they also be in Us so that the world may believe that You have sent Me. 22 I have given them the glory that You gave Me, that they may be one as We are One: 23 I in them and You in Me. May they be brought to complete unity to let the world know that You sent Me and have loved them even as You have loved Me. 24 Father, I want those You have given Me to be with Me where I am, and to see My glory, the glory you have given Me because You loved Me before the creation of the world. 25 Righteous Father, though the world does not know You, I know You, and they know that You have sent Me. 26 I have made You known to them, and will continue to make You known in order that the love You have for Me may be in them and that I Myself may be in them."

Jesus specifically prayed for unity three times here. In verse eleven He made and extraordinary request. The appeal Jesus makes here is that you and I would be in unity to the same extent that He and His Father were. It is hard for me to comprehend such a request. How could this be possible? We have such a hard time with unity. How could Jesus ever think we could be united, just as He and the Father? Knowing this is the desire of Jesus should make it our desire as well. Also knowing that Jesus has prayed this to His Father should give us the faith to know that, whether we can comprehend it or not, it will come to pass! The more you walk out unity in your daily life, the richer your prayer life will be.

2. Father

Luke 15: 11 Jesus continued: "There was a man who had two sons. 12 The younger one said to his father, 'Father, give me my share of the estate.' So he divided his property between them. 13 Not long after that, the younger son got together all he had, set off for a distant country and there squandered his wealth in wild living. 14 After he had spent everything, there was a severe famine in that whole country, and he began to be in need. 15 So he went and hired himself out to a citizen of that country, who sent him to his fields to feed pigs. 16 He longed to fill his stomach with the pods that the pigs were eating, but no one gave him anything. 17 "When he came to his senses, he said, 'How many of my father's hired men have food to spare, and here I am starving to death! 18 I will set out and go back to my father and say to him: Father, I have sinned against heaven and against you. 19 I am no longer worthy to be called your son; make me like one of your hired men.' 20 So he got up and went to his father. "But while he was still a long way off, his father saw him and was filled with compassion for him; he ran to his son, threw his arms around him and kissed him. 21 "The son said to him, 'Father, I have sinned against heaven and against you. I am no longer worthy to be called your son. ' 22 "But the father said to his servants, 'Quick! Bring the best robe and put it on him. Put a ring on his finger and sandals on his feet. 23 Bring the fattened calf and kill it. Let's have a feast and celebrate. 24 For this son of mine was dead and is alive again; he was lost and is found.' So they began to celebrate. 25 "Meanwhile, the older son was in the field. When he came near the house, he heard music and dancing. 26 So he called one of the servants and asked him what was going on. 27 'Your brother has come,' he replied, 'and your father has killed the fattened calf because he has him back safe and sound.' 28 "The older brother became angry and refused to go in. So his father went out and pleaded with him. 29 But he answered his father, 'Look! All these years I've been slaving for you and never disobeyed your orders. Yet you never gave me even a young goat so I could celebrate with my friends. 30 But when this son of yours who has squandered your property with prostitutes comes home, you kill the fattened calf for him!' 31 " 'My son,' the father said, 'you are always with me, and everything I have is yours. 32 But we had to celebrate and be glad, because this brother of yours was dead and is alive again; he was lost and is found.' "

This story is often referred to as the parable of the prodigal son. It is true that one of the main characters in the story is the prodigal son, but many people over look the other son. To fully understand this parable it is important that you put it into context. This will help you understand the full point Jesus is trying to get across. He directed this story at the Pharisees and the teachers of the law. They were upset because Jesus was spending time with the people that religious people looked down on. In this parable Jesus was comparing these religious leaders to the envious son. These men were discontent. There was something missing in their lives in spite of how hard they had worked. They were exactly like the brother who was envious of the love his father had lavished on his sibling.

The lives of both brothers demonstrate the mistake of failing to walk in their father's provision and care. Notice what the envious brother said to his father in verse twenty-nine. "All these years I have slaved for you." This man was not enjoying his walk with the father. Perhaps he was trying to prove how much better he was than his brother. Whatever the case, his perspective on life was not one of a blessed favored son. This poor man had been deceived into working like a slave. This was not what his father wanted for him. When he accused his father of not even giving him a goat, he was over looking the fact that, just for the asking this same father had given his brother the full inheritance! The key to a rich full and happy life for both sons can be found in the father's response. "You are always with me. Everything that I have is your's. Both sons missed this. Both sons failed to comprehend or walk in the fullness of their father's love. Both sons had lived a discontent life of want, when everything they desired was there for them.

How would your life change if your father was the wealthiest and most powerful man in the country? If you were the center of his life and you knew that he would do anything in his power to bless you, would this change your perspective on life? The fact is that God the Father loves you. You are infinitely valuable to Him. He loves you with a perfect and full love. Nothing you can do will make Him love you more or less. He has said to you, "Everything that I have is yours." To say, "Our Father" does not do much for your prayer life. Aw, but to live out, or to walk out the truth is quite another thing. When you begin to walk in the truth, that God is my Father, your prayer life will never again be burdensome. It will be a constant joy. It will be a beautiful conversation with your loving Father God, which never comes to a conclusion.

3. Which art it heaven

This part of your prayer life has to do with perspective. How do things look from God's vantage point? Job lived out this truth for us. Job demonstrated his understanding of this truth as he walked through adversities. Although Job complained at times, in the end he acknowledged that God was in heaven. When you acknowledge this in your life, you are saying that God say see and know things from His heavenly vantage point that we cannot see here and now. Take some time and read the book of Job with this in mind.

In Isaiah 55: 8 "My thoughts are completely different from yours," says the LORD. "And My ways are far beyond anything you could imagine. 9 For just as the heavens are higher than the earth, so are My ways higher than your ways and My thoughts higher than your thoughts."

Here is a practical way I have found to make this truth part of my daily walk. I look at the issue before me and ask this question. How will this look 100 years from today? When you ask this question it will often make big things look very small and small things look very big. Here is an example. A few years ago I was able to take my wife and two children to Cambodia on a mission trip. The financial preparation for this was difficult to say the least. Two days before we were to leave I was at work. At the time I was working at the detention center for at risk teens that I spoke about earlier. The students and the staff always watched me. I have always been very public with my faith. They wanted to see if I practiced what I preached. While I was at work I received a call from my wife telling me that the transmission our van had gone bad. We were stretched to the max in our finances. This was a disaster! The repair would cost nearly $2,000. I looked at this disaster and asked myself, "How will this look in 100 years?" This did not make the problem go away by any means. It simply gave me the right perspective to deal with the situation. I had no idea how it would work out, but I knew that if I looked at it the way my Father was looking at it, everything would eventually work out. I am still driving that van today. The thing that looked huge that day is now a memory. 100 years from today it will be forgotten. The impact my action had on the students that day did not look all that big. As I listened to my wife tell me about the extent of the damage to our car, I was not thinking about the impact this might have on those around me. What they thought about the matter seemed very small. Several months latter as one of my students was preparing to go back home she told me how much it impacted her life. She had heard me talk about faith. I had told her that God would take care of her. As she watched me walk out what I had taught her, she made up her mind to make my God her God! The transmission looked huge. Today it looks very small. What a young girl thought about the matter looked unimportant, but 100 years from today it will still be a big deal.

This part of the prayer tells us that from heaven's perspective we always win. We will outlive every problem. Our enemy's resources are limited. Our resources come from heaven and are eternal! This truth did not make all of Job's problems go away, but it gave him the strength to fight and win in the day of war.

4. Hallowed be Thy Name

To hallow something simply means to set it apart as something special; holy or sacred. The Pharisees of every time period have done this with their lips, but not with their life. Talk is cheap and actions speak louder than words! To hallow God's name you must first understand that when you were born again and became a child of God He gave you His name. You are now a Christian. As such you represent Christ. A bad son or daughter can tarnish the family name by the way he lives. In contrast, a good son or daughter can hallow, or set apart as special, the family name with an honorable life. You hallow God's name by showing up to work on time and always doing a good job. You hallow God's name by being a good neighbor. You hallow God's name in every detail of your daily life. When you live the kind of life that makes other people stop and take notice and when that life points to the grace and mercy of God, then you are living a life or prayer!

5. Thy Kingdom Come

Matthew 6: 31 "So don't worry about having enough food or drink or clothing. 32 Why be like the pagans who are so deeply concerned about these things? Your heavenly Father already knows all your needs, 33 and He will give you all you need from day to day if you live for Him and make the Kingdom of God your primary concern." (NLT)

The King James Version of this verse thirty-three is very well-known. It reads, "Seek ye first the Kingdom." If a person is not careful this will convey a wrong message. If I am going on a long trip, first I fill my gas tank. Filling the gas tank is not my primary concern. I am filling my gas tank so I can get to the destination. The destination is my primary concern. The selfish nature in all of us will view Jesus' instruction in this passage as, first we seek the kingdom then we get the stuff. This may prompt us to work very hard at kingdom things for a season, but our motivation is wrong. In order of priorities we are doing God's work, but in order of value we have other things in mind. You can see evidence of this as you look around at our churches today. People will have a crisis come and shake up their lives. In a broken state they reach out to God and begin to attend church. As time passes and their lives stabilize they start to drift away from the things of God. These people were never truly looking for change. They were looking for relief.

To seek a particular kingdom is to seek the King! If I am sincerely seeking God's Kingdom then my true affection will be for its King, Who is Jesus. When this happens, the way I spend my time, the friends I have, the way I spend my money, even where I choose to live will all be governed by my desire to see Jesus' Kingdom established. This lifestyle is a battle cry! When you live in one kingdom and cry out for a different king, you will find yourself at war. When your lifestyle demonstrates that you are serious about making Jesus king, you will be in conflict with much of the world around you. Jesus told His disciples that even as the world had hated Him, it would hate them too. Paul warned us about becoming friends with the world.

In John 12:25, Jesus tells us that those who love their lives will lose them, but those who despise their lives in this world would keep it. Why would I want to keep what I despise. What Jesus was saying here is set your priorities. When the Kingdom of God becomes you primary concern, you are going to discover some things you really wanted are no longer important to you. Other things that you wanted will be given to you. However, when you receive them, you will not be distracted by them. This will be true because you weren't just saying, "Thy Kingdom come." Thy Kingdom come is your lifestyle.

6. Thy will be done on earth as it is in heaven

One of the most visible aspects of the life of Jesus was His motivation to do the will of the Father. He constantly pointed out that His words and actions were governed by the will of the Father. Our failure to do this is often brought about by our lack of faith in God. Any time I choose my will over His, I am saying, by my actions, that I believe I can do better for myself. Satan has succeeded in convincing us that God is holding out on us. The prominent mindset for many young people today can be summed up this way. I will settle down some day, but for now I want to have some fun. Too often the cost for that fun is overwhelming and most often the truth is; it wasn't all that much fun either. This mindset underestimates heaven and fails to understand that God is a perfect and loving Father. Any good father wants to give his child everything good. A good father only withholds what will hurt the child. When he withholds ice cream, he is not being mean or trying to prove a point. It is because too much ice cream is not good for the child. It is human nature to fear that giving up my will and holding only to God's will is going to short change me. Consider the disciples. Jesus was teaching them to put the Kingdom of God first. Their body language must have given Him insight into their fears. In Luke 12:32 Jesus said, "So don't be afraid, little flock. For it gives your Father great happiness to give you the Kingdom." God's will for us is heaven on earth. He delights in giving us every good thing. When we believe this in our heart, it will be a natural part of our daily walk to seek God's will in every detail of our lives.

7. Give us this day our daily bread

When I make this a part of my lifestyle, I am trusting God for all my provisions.

Luke 11: 10 "For everyone who asks, receives. Everyone who seeks, finds. And the door is opened to everyone who knocks. 11 You fathers -- if your children ask for a fish, do you give them a snake instead? 12 Or if they ask for an egg, do you give them a scorpion? Of course not! 13 If you sinful people know how to give good gifts to your children, how much more will your heavenly Father give the Holy Spirit to those who ask Him."

When we believe this, we will stop struggling with things on our own. We will stop and seek God for our daily needs.

8. Forgive us our debts as we forgive our debtors

There is so much packed into this one short line. Forgiveness is an obvious point in this line and must be a part of every Christian's lifestyle. What is Christianity without forgiveness? Remember the first component in this prayer? It was unity. Look at how this theme carries through the prayer. He we are on the eighth component and we see the words "us" and "our." There are two groups of people here. The word "us" refers to the Christian family of God. We are often in need of forgiveness. When was the last time you approached the Father and repented for sins other than your own? Forgive us, is a constant theme throughout the Old Testament. The book of Micah is largely a record of Micah repenting for the sins of his nation, Israel. The sins he was repenting were not personally his. He joined in unity with his nation and repented and cried out for forgiveness. What a powerful concept! If we would join with our brothers and sisters who have stumbled and cried out; "Lord please forgive us," it would lift us out of our judgmental state of mind. When the Holy Spirit revealed this truth to me, I found myself looking at things differently. I used to criticize Hollywood all the time. I used to condemn my country for all the abortions and other immoral activity. I felt separate or detached as though I was not at all responsible. The truth is that the Christians in America bear a certain amount of responsibility for these things.

2 Chronicles 7:14 "If My people, which are called by My name, shall humble themselves, and pray, and seek My face, and turn from their wicked ways; then will I hear from heaven, and will forgive their sin, and will heal their land." (KJV)

This verse is reflective. If God's people were humbly praying and seeking God's face, there would be healing in our land. God is the One Who said this in 2 Chronicles 7:14. He is not a man that He should lie. What we have done in America is judge and criticize. What we have failed to do is pray. Our prayer here in America should be, "Lord forgive our apathy and our misplaced priorities and forgive those people in Hollywood. Forgive our political leaders." Far too often we are like Jonah who wanted God's judgment to fall instead of having a desire for repentance of the wicked.

9. Lead us not into temptation, but deliver us from evil

This line was the most difficult for me to understand when I first began looking into this revelation. Why would Jesus instruct me to ask God not to do something, when it is clear in Scripture God would never tempt me to do evil?

James 1; 13 "Let no man say when he is tempted, I am tempted of God: for God cannot be tempted with evil, neither tempteth He any man." (KJV)

The first part of the answer is this. This line is not a request. This entire prayer and the lifestyle it promotes is an agreement. As I begin to walk this prayer out in my daily life, I come into harmony with God's will for my life. The first two words establish God as the leader. When we submit to God's leadership He will take us away from temptation and deliver us from all evil.

Every moral failure, every addiction that has ever formed, every time you looked back with regret at the devastation sin has brought to your life; there is a single deception that preceded the breakdown. The thought that produced the action that brought the damage was this; "I can handle this." A wise person says, "There but for the grace of God go I." The proud person says, "Others might not be able to handle this temptation, but I can. I can go just so far and stop. After all, I would never…" In eight years of prison ministry, I met hundreds of men who could say, "I never thought I would do the things I did to get here." The pastors who fell into adultery all have one thing in common. The gateway that led them to their moral failure was the thought, "I would never…" This is a prideful thought. The humble thought is, "Lord I am weak. If I am placed in the wrong environment, I will fail." A wise pastor would have said to his secretary, "We cannot work late and be alone. There is temptation there and even though it looks ever so small now, we will follow the leading of the Holy Spirit." The Holy Spirit will always lead you away from temptation. I wrote a poem a few years ago, while dealing with some students who were trying to escape the party life.

The Party

By Allen Porter

The plans have been made. The money is spent
and finally the moment arrives
The people show up with smiles on their faces
expecting the time of their lives.
The beer is on ice. The drugs are in place
and everything's ready to go.
It's been a long week. Let the party begin.
If only these people could know.
The price for this party is more than they reckon.
They'll pay for it all of their lives.
With innocence lost and trust that's been broken;
Events that cut deeper than knives.
They know in their hearts they'll do things they shouldn't.
But the pleasure it calls them by name.
Addiction forms and relationships shatter
And some will regret that they came.
Still others may leave and find their way home,
Thinking everything's gonna be fine.
But confidence gained is based on deception,
So they'll keep on crossing the line.
In all of the ages not one single person
Said addiction will be my fate.
So party by party they say, "One more time."
And realize only too late
The seeds have been sown and the harvest is due.
The yield will hurt family and friends.
To watch their beloved falter and struggle
Till finally their lives find an end.

The sin that calls your name may not be a party. It may not be alcohol
or drugs. Regardless what the temptation is, part of the deceit will be
that you think that you can control it. You cannot control a sin any more
than you can control death. The Bible tells us that the wages of sin is

death. Satan loves to whisper to us about sins without consequence, but remember, he is the father of lies and cannot speak the truth.

A person who does not know how to swim can say with confidence, "I will never drown." He will be successful in his claim as long as he has a healthy fear of the water. If he gets overly confident there is possibility of drowning. As long as he acknowledges his weakness he is 100% safe.

When you make this component part of your daily walk, you will seek out accountability. You will realize your weakness and God's strength. This knowledge will cause you to be dependent on His leadership at all times. When you do this you will find yourself in agreement with the Holy Spirit and He will, in fact, lead you and deliver you!

10. For Thine is the Kingdom, the power and the glory forever

This line is not found in the early manuscripts. It is believed by many scholars that this line was added by translators at a later date. It does reaffirm the line three through six. It reminds us what our priorities should be. He reminds us Who is in charge. When we make this line part of our daily walk, we will be like Jesus. When every moment of our daily life is about affirming this truth, our lives will be in harmony with the will of God! We will be a light to the world around us as the very power of God overshadows us. In the hard times, people will see strength and honor and a peace that passes understanding. In the good times people will see the favor of Almighty God as blessings flow out from our life. Selfish ambition will be a thing of the past. We will not focus only on the temporary day-to-day events of life, but on the eternal glory of God, which is our destiny!

The most difficult trial for anyone is the death of a close loved one. Yet, even at the graveside of our beloved this truth brings a deep peace and joy, which will abide long after the sorrow has subsided. This is a testimony that lifts high our King, Jesus! As we exalt King Jesus, we rock the gates of hell in this day of war!

11. Amen

In the minds of many this word means, the end. It is a way of wrapping up or concluding a prayer. However, we have learned that the fervent effective prayer is the walk of prayer. Our prayer is the conversation that never comes to a conclusion.

Once again, in most early manuscripts the word, "amen" does not appear. However this word was a very common word in the Jewish vocabulary. The word is powerful. The most common definition is, "so be it." It means the matter is settled.

Jesus demonstrates the lifestyle of amen in this familiar story beginning in Mark Chapter 4, verse 35 "As evening came, Jesus said to His disciples, 'Let's cross to the other side of the lake.' 36 He was already in the boat, so they started out, leaving the crowds behind (although other boats followed). 37 But soon a fierce storm arose. High waves began to break into the boat until it was nearly full of water. 38 Jesus was sleeping at the back of the boat with His head on a cushion. Frantically they woke Him up, shouting, 'Teacher, don't you even care that we are going to drown?' 39 When He woke up, He rebuked the wind and said to the water, 'Quiet down!' Suddenly the wind stopped, and there was a great calm. 40 And He asked them, 'Why are you so afraid? Do you still not have faith in Me?' 41 And they were filled with awe and said among themselves, 'Who is this man, that even the wind and waves obey Him?' "

Before getting into the boat, Jesus had spent a considerable amount of time teaching about faith. Over the years I have heard many sermons on this passage. In most sermons the preacher inferred that the disciples should have used their faith to calm the storm. I do not believe that is the case. I do not believe their faith was sufficient. They did have a degree of faith in Jesus. Even though they accused Him of not caring if they all died, they still had enough faith to call on Him for help. If only they had a full understanding of with Whom they were in the boat. This was Jesus Christ, the Son of God! He had made a statement before the journey began, "Let's cross to the other side of the lake." Then He laid down and fell asleep. The storm did not wake Him. He was not at all concerned about the storm. The storm was irrelevant! Jesus was fully God and fully man. He had made His will known. We are going to the other side. When He said this, it was settled. Jesus Christ, the Son of the Living God was not going to drown at sea! He knew this! If the disciples would have responded instead of reacting, they could have come to this same revelation. They could have laid down next to Jesus and slept through the storm. That is walking out the truth of amen.

Conclusion

James 1: 22 And remember, it is a message to obey, not just to listen to. If you don't obey, you are only fooling yourself.

My hope is that the time and money you have invested in this book has brought some added knowledge and reinforced some things you already knew. It is my greatest hope that you feel empowered to fight for lost souls. As you do this every other blessing in life will come you way.

As a final word of encourage let me urge you to stay on the offense! Jesus has already conquered the power of sin and death and He has made us more than conquerors in His name. This does not mean that we will not slip up on occasion and find ourselves in a defensive posture, but when this happens, repent and get back into your offensive position. Some where there is a lost soul waiting for you to answer your call to Christ and set them free.

The armor of God is not tailored just to fit pastors. It is not just for missionaries. God's armor is for every believer. If He has provided you with armor, He has also called you to fight.

People do not come to Christ because of dynamic worship services or great preaching. The Bible clearly tells us that these things are foolishness to those who are lost. People come to know Christ as they see and experience His power in the life of some one they know and respect. Some where in your life some one is watching you. They are taking note of how you handle crisis. They are watching to see if there is anything in your life that is missing in theirs.

Several years ago I was running a small business. I had a group of sales reps who I had hired and trained. We had all moved to a new city and set up shop and things were not going well. One night one of the sales reps came to me came to me in tears. He told me he just wanted to make enough money to get back home. From a distance another one of our sales team was watching and listening. I told the disheartened sales rep that I would personally ride with him the next day and that we would raise the funds needed to get him back home. I then climbed up on the roof of the office complex where we worked and prayed. I was worried that I would not be able to live up to my promise. The next day this man and I went out and by noon we were back in the office with the needed provision to get him back home. The man who had watched from afar came over and said, "You prayed last night didn't you?" This man had often mocked my faith. He loved to party and he wanted nothing to do with any religion. I answered his question and we went on with our business. A number of years later after we had all gone our separate ways I met this man who had mocked my faith and discovered that he and his wife were serving Jesus. They had reached a point of brokenness. Their marriage was on the rocks. Nothing was going right and this man remembered me praying that night. He remembered the victory! He told me how one night when he and his wife were at the end of the resources he said to his wife. "Remember Allen Porter and that time he prayed…" There without a preacher or an alter call they called on the name of the Lord Jesus and he saved them.

Living a life of victory is a great way to witness! A life of victory in the eyes of Jesus is far different than what the world perceives as victory. No one cheered the day we made the sale and sent the weary sales rep back home. I had completely forgotten it till I reconnected with my old friend. But the testimony lived on and produced fruit!

Remember Jesus was and is the greatest Spiritual Warrior of all time. He came to destroy the works of the devil. As you lay down this book look around. Can you identify any works of the devil? If so, wait upon the Lord and He will call you to arms! He has a special mission. One that you are uniquely qualified for. He will give you the grace along with His mighty armor. As you destroy the works of the devil you will be setting the captives free. This is life at it fullest as we serve side by side with one another under the banner of our King Jesus in this day of war!